Chefs A' Field Kids on the Farm

the companion book to the award-winning public television series

Chefs A' Field: Kids on the Farm Companion Book
Copyright (c)2007 by Warner Hanson Television

This book is based on *Chefs A' Field: Kids on the Farm*, the third season of the acclaimed and award-winning public television series. Tune in to *Chefs A' Field: Kids on the Farm* on your local public television series.

All rights reserved. No portion of this book may be reproduced—mechanically, electronically, or by any other means without the written permission of Warner Hanson Television.

All photos in this book are reproduced from HDTV frame-grabs sourced from from the series extensive footage. All photos © Warner Hanson Television and Chefs A' Field.

Published, designed, and created by Warner Hanson Television
Washington, D.C.

WARNERHANSON.COM

Assistance provided by Star Print Brokers ~ Bellevue, WA
Printed in South Korea.

ISBN: 978-1-60402-415-9

Chefs A' Field is a co-production of:
Warner Hanson Television & KCTS/Seattle Public Television.

The public television series is distributed by American Public Television.

Chefs A' Field ©2007 Warner Hanson Television & KCTS/Seattle Public Television. All rights reserved.

CHEFSAFIELD.COM

Chefs A' Field Kids on the Farm
the companion book to the award-winning public television series

compiled & created by
Warner Hanson Television

recipes by
Richard Sandoval
Michael Mina
Robert Wiedmaier
Mitchell & Steven Rosenthal
Bruce Sherman
Joseph Wrede
Cathal Armstrong
John Besh
David Bull
Michel Nischan
Bill Telepan
Jason Wilson

contributions by
Joel Salatin
Marsha Rhems I Judy Mannes
Chris Warner I Heidi Hanson

photography by
Tim Murray I Mark Thalman
Rich Joy I Chris Warner

edited by
Pat Mallinson

based on the public television series co-produced by
Warner Hanson Television & KCTS/Seattle Public Television

the award-winning public television series

James Beard Foundation Award
Best National Television Cooking Show
Best Television Cooking Special

CINE Award
2005 CINE Golden Eagle Award
2006 CINE Golden Eagle Award

White House News Photographers Award
Best Documentary – Silver Award

Chicago International Film Festival
Hugo Gold Award

Food & Wine Magazine
Tastemaker Award

acknowledgments

Warner Hanson Television would like to thank the very special individuals who have been a part of the past three seasons of *Chefs A' Field*—Especially our families, close friends, and viewers, whose encouragement has made thirty-nine episodes of this series possible.

The thirteen magnificent chefs and their children who endured everything from endless dusty roads and scorching summer heat to 3:00 A.M. wake-up calls and icy artic waters in search of great ingredients. These chefs truly believe in sustainability and supporting their local communities as well as educating their children on food and the environment. Thank you for all of your time, thoughtfulness, and physical exertion.

Our biggest thanks go to all the farmers, fishermen, and foragers who work tirelessly everyday, rain or shine, to bring delicious, clean, and nutritious food to our tables. In an age of dirty, globalized food, we thank you for growing and catching clean food in our local communities. Your dedication will resonate for many generations to come.

And finally, we give great thanks to our our series sponsors and partners, who have had the great vision to make *Chefs A' Field: Kids on the Farm* possible: Whole Foods Market, Full Circle Food, The Park Foundation, The Wallace Genetic Foundation, Seeds of Change, Spoons Across America, and KCTS Television.

Thank you for being a part of this great adventure.

table of contents

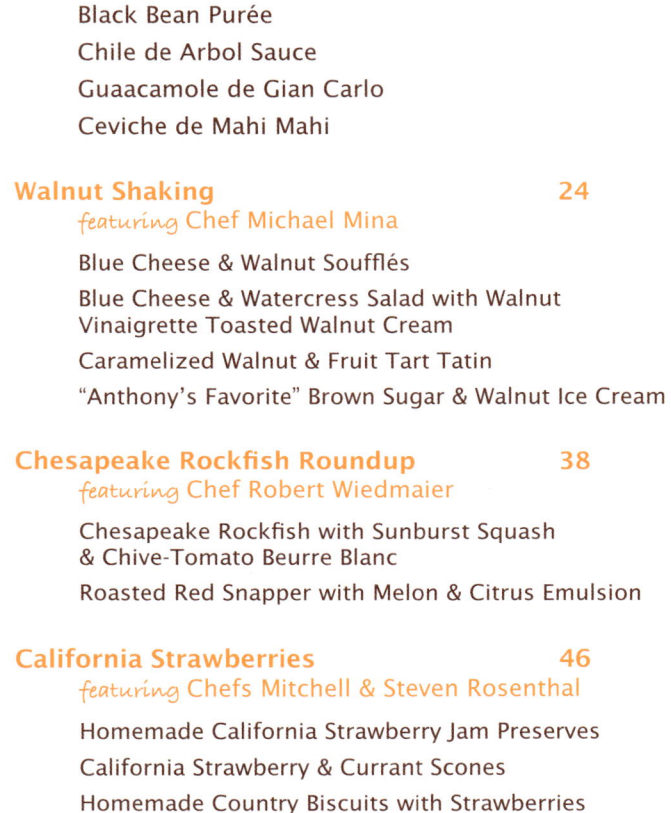

Where has the Courtship gone?   8
foreword by Joel Salatin of Polyface Farm

In Search of Avocados   12
featuring Chef Richard Sandoval

- Piramide de Res
- Black Bean Purée
- Chile de Arbol Sauce
- Guaacamole de Gian Carlo
- Ceviche de Mahi Mahi

Walnut Shaking   24
featuring Chef Michael Mina

- Blue Cheese & Walnut Soufflés
- Blue Cheese & Watercress Salad with Walnut Vinaigrette Toasted Walnut Cream
- Caramelized Walnut & Fruit Tart Tatin
- "Anthony's Favorite" Brown Sugar & Walnut Ice Cream

Chesapeake Rockfish Roundup   38
featuring Chef Robert Wiedmaier

- Chesapeake Rockfish with Sunburst Squash & Chive-Tomato Beurre Blanc
- Roasted Red Snapper with Melon & Citrus Emulsion

California Strawberries   46
featuring Chefs Mitchell & Steven Rosenthal

- Homemade California Strawberry Jam Preserves
- California Strawberry & Currant Scones
- Homemade Country Biscuits with Strawberries & Prosciutto

Artisan Chèvre   58
featuring Chef Bruce Sherman

- Apple & Chèvre Double-Stuffed Delicata Squash Boats
- Apple-Leek Soup with Herbed Goat Cheese Gnocchi & Nest of Fresh Spinach

Seed Saving & Heirloom Veggies   68
featuring Chef Joseph Wrede

- Six-Tomato Summer Gazpacho
- Herbaceous Fried Shrimp

Shrimp Boat on the Bayou   80
featuring Chef John Besh

- The Besh Louisiana Barbeque Shrimp
- Louisiana Shrimp & Grits with Andouille
- Louisiana Shrimp Stock
- Tempura Gulf Shrimp with Hoisin Salad

Fields, Not Feedlots   92
featuring Chef Cathal Armstrong

- New World Braised Pork & Beans
- Roasted Breast of Polyface Farm Chicken with Swiss Chard & Wild Virginia Chanterelles

Hill Country Venison   100
featuring Chef David Bull

- Slow-Cooked Wild Venison Stew
- Roasted Rack of Broken Arrow Venison with Grilled Trumpet Mushrooms
- Bacon Horseradish-Turnip Purée
- Seared Venison Loin with Blackberry-Fig Jam & Braised Romaine

Winter Bay Scallops   110
featuring Chefs Michel Nischan

- Taylor Bay Scallop Farrotto
- Green Apple Sweet Scallop Lollipops

New York Dairy   118
featuring Chef Bill Telepan

- Cauliflower with Egg Noodles, Farmer's Cheese & Black Pepper
- Leah's Favorite "Vanilla Pudding Sunde Surprise" with Caramelized Oranges & Cookies

Wild Foraging & Island Duck Eggs   130
featuring Chef Jason Wilson

- Brioche French Toast with Maple Blossoms & Salmonberry Flower Cream
- Wild Watercress Hollandaise
- Dungeness Crab & Wild Nettle Gratin with Grandma's Poached Duck Eggs

Supporting Sustainability   144

People & Places   152

foreword

Where has the courtship gone?

BY JOEL SALATIN
POLYFACE FARM SWOOPE, VIRGINIA

Next to the act of marriage, taking in the fuel that provides energy for our bodies is perhaps the most intimate thing most of us ever do.

After all, we're taking this food in, ingesting it, assimilating it, metabolizing it: It becomes a part of us, flesh of our flesh, bone of our bones.

And yet modern industrial agriculture has dehumanized and de-romanticized everything leading up to this intimate experience. Most food production creates noise, pollution, odors, and unsightliness that push people away. America now has more prisoners than farmers.

What does not exist anymore is the knowledge, relationship, and romance necessary to fully enjoy the sensual experience of dining—the tastes, textures, and sights on the table before us.

Where is the courtship? Where is the "dating" that creates the authenticity and heightens the pleasure of the dining experience?

In the modern quest for cheaper, faster, fatter, bigger, we've removed accountability from the food relationship. We've eliminated the nurturing and instead created prostitution food—food that is owned, produced, prepared, and distributed by the shortest-sighted bidder. Indeed, dining has become less fulfilling than a one-night stand, and just as degrading to the producers, preparers, and patrons.

Enter *Chefs A' Field*, a celebration that applauds food relationships and the web of accountability that necessarily surrounds a healing, healthy food system.

What a captivating pleasure it is to see the connections between farmer and plate. As food sculptors, chefs bring to our food culture an artisanal passion that honors good land stewardship, plant and animal husbandry, and the best culinary traditions.

Good chefs are perhaps the finest arbiters in the ongoing debate over whether food should be produced through natural biological processes or through the large-scale mechanical processes of industrial agriculture. For, when looking for memorable dining experiences, even the most die-hard defenders of industrially produced fare will seek chefs who patronize local, humane, grass-based, ecologically sensitive farmers over their factory-farm counterparts. The *Chefs A' Field* television series and cookbooks bring into America's psyche the magic that occurs when exceptional producers interact with artisans of the dining experience.

The dance that inevitably ensues from symbiotic farmer-chef connections extends to families, communities, and ultimately even earthworms. Capturing this choreography on film and through the written word brings to every reader, every observer, the beauty of food well produced and well prepared.

All of us can and should aspire to appreciate, to the depths of our soul, the aesthetic pleasure surrounding this kind of food integrity. Our relationship with food forms a tapestry into which each of us weaves a portion of the landscape our children will inherit, one bite at a time.

Enjoy these food relationships for their passion. Enjoy them for their integrity. But enjoy them, especially, for their rich contributions to a hurried, harried culture seeking meaning and purpose.

Chefs A' Field presents food for the body, mind, and spirit.

Please partake. Often. Fully. Gratefully.

how to use this book

Everybody into the Kitchen

Chefs A' Field: Kids on the Farm is meant to be enjoyed by adults and children together. The recipes are written for adults, with "kid-friendly" ideas for involving the entire family.

The dishes contained within are not "kid" meals, but *real* dishes—recipes served up to discriminating customers in some of America's very best restaurants. But here, they are given new life. Each chef's special touches make them interesting to eat, and family-friendly to prepare.

This book is more than just a cookbook. It's an exploration of food and how food connects us to its sources, to culture, to history, to the environment, and even to math and science. It is a resource for learning, engaging, and exploring your food and your natural world.

Activities in each chapter explore such questions as: What does color tell you about a food? Can salt make food sweeter? What did Christopher Columbus put on his spaghetti? Is a cucumber a fruit or a vegetable? How do you milk a cow? Can you cut an onion without tears? When is a cup not a cup? Do hard-cooked eggs spoil faster than fresh eggs?

The activities appeal to kids' curiosity—as well as adults'—and their fondness for experimenting as they shop, cook, and eat.

Food is an integral part of our lives: a means for bringing people and families together. We hope that you will read, shop, cook, dine, and engage in food with your family—and your community.

It is our hope that this book will inspire you to explore—and engage in discussion—with your family as you gather together around great food.

Enjoy!

about the series

Chefs A' Field is a 39-part public television series unlike any other.

Chefs A' Field has won numerous awards and considerable critical acclaim while pioneering the use of HDTV in the cooking genre. It also has helped create a new approach to food on television by taking viewers out of the kitchen and out to the source.

The series is not merely about cooking, but about *passion*—passion in growing and preparing the food that fuels our bodies and our souls. Around the world, we meet the people and see the places that define our diverse food culture.

The third season of *Chefs A' Field*, *Kids on the Farm*, offers a new batch of culinary adventures for all ages as America's best chefs—*and their kids*—venture out to farms, fishing boats, and ranches for a look at where great food comes from. Together, the chefs and their children go in search of fresh ingredients for unique local specialties, interacting with those who grow and gather them.

Television viewers and diners alike have marveled at the incredible food that the award-winning chefs from *Chefs A' Field* have created over the years. Through this companion cookbook, readers can step behind the scenes and get their hands on recipes, shopping tips, gardening advice, family-friendly cooking ideas, and other secrets from the series.

From shrimping in a Louisiana bayou to heirloom tomato-sampling in Taos, New Mexico, to cheese-making in the rolling hills of southern Wisconsin, the chefs and children featured in *Chefs A' Field: Kids on the Farm* explore the many faces and places of America's diverse food landscape. Exclusive glimpses into America's finest restaurants are combined with family-friendly cooking lessons as chefs and children return to the kitchen to create wonderful dishes ranging from Chesapeake Rockfish with Sunburst Squash & Chive-Tomato Beurre Blanc to California Strawberry & Currant Scones to Green Apple Sweet Scallop Lollipops.

In each part of *Chefs A' Field: Kids on the Farm*, viewers and readers alike will discover why thoughtful agricultural practices make a difference in how foods taste and hold their nutritional value, while learning valuable tips and ideas for cooking with their own families.

Chefs A' Field: Kids on the Farm travels to Michoacán, Mexico; San Francisco; Washington, D.C.; Chicago; Taos; New Orleans; Alexandria, Virginia; Austin, Texas; Westport, Connecticut; New York City; and Seattle. Through these journeys, we meet chefs, producers and purveyors representing the full spectrum of our diverse food world.

Come along on this culinary adventure as we discover the stories of the people and places that define great food.

In Search of Avocados

featuring

CHEF RICHARD SANDOVAL
  MODERN MEXICAN RESTAURANTS
   ISLA LAS VEGAS, NEVADA
   LA SANDÍA DENVER, COLORADO
   MAYA NEW YORK / SAN FRANCISCO / DUBAI
   PAMPANO NEW YORK, NEW YORK
   ZENGO DENVER / WASHINGTON, D.C.
   TAMAYO DENVER, COLORADO

ANTONIO VILLASEÑOR
  LA MESA ALTA FARM MICHOACÁN, MEXICO

Richard Sandoval and his nine-year-old son Gian Carlo venture to the chef's birthplace to find the indigenous ingredients that inspired a budding four-star chef decades ago.

Among the ancient mountains of Michoacán, Mexico, their travels take them through ancient villages and dramatic landscapes. They even saddle up for a horseback ride to the top of a volcano for an understanding of where this region gets its rich soil.

Back down in the valley, where the lush green canopy of avocado trees cools the air, Chef Sandoval and Gian Carlo get their hands on "green gold," also known as the Hass avocado.

Avocado grower Antonio Villaseñor takes them on a tour of his family's orchards and offers a lesson in just how to pick the perfect avocado.

Some of the trees are over three hundred years old, and young Gian Carlo doesn't hesitate to climb one of them as part of his adventure.

Back on solid ground, Chef Sandoval and son sample the avocado for inspiration.

Throughout their adventure, the natural beauty of Mexico shines on them as they celebrate the folklore, gastronomy, and traditions of this majestic region.

Chef Richard Sandoval
Piramide de Res
GRILLED SKIRT STEAK WITH ONIONS, BLACK BEAN PURÉE, AND CHILE DE ARBOL SAUCE

INGREDIENTS
4 large slices skirt steak *(about 5 ounces each)*, trimmed
1 tablespoon canola oil
4 large slices white onion
1½ tablespoons lemon juice
Salt, *to taste*
White pepper, *to taste*
1 tablespoon Maggi® Seasoning Sauce
4 slices tomato, ¼-inch slices
1 cup Black Bean Purée
 (See accompanying recipe.)
1 cup Guacamole de Gian Carlo
 (See accompanying recipe.)
1 cup crisp tortilla strips
4 ounces Chile de Arbol Sauce
 (See accompanying recipe.)

PREPARATION
Pound the skirt steak to a thickness of about ¼ inch. Preheat the grill or broiler to high temperature.

In a large skillet, heat the oil. Remove the pan from the heat and add the onion slices. Sauté them over medium heat until softened and lightly golden, approximately 8 to 10 minutes. Remove from the heat and season with the lemon juice, adding salt, pepper, and the Maggi sauce. Set aside.

Season the tomato slices with a pinch of salt and pepper. Grill or broil the tomato until softened, about 2 minutes per side.

Season the steak with salt and pepper. Grill or broil until desired doneness—2 minutes per side for medium-rare. Let stand for 2 minutes, and then cut against the grain into thin slices.

ON THE PLATE
Spoon ¼ cup of the Black Bean Purée in the center of each of 4 dinner plates. Place a tomato slice on top of the purée, followed by a slice of the sautéed onion and a pile of the sliced steak, creating a "tower," as desired. Spoon ¼ cup of the Guacamole de Gian Carlo over the meat. Place crisp tortilla strips on top, and if desired, drizzle the plate with the Chile de Arbol Sauce.

YIELD ~ 4 SERVINGS

SOURCING NOTES
Maggi Seasoning Sauce is a common ingredient in Mexican and Asian cooking. It is a combination of salt, spices, and pepper that can be compared to soy sauce in its taste and consistency. Maggi Seasoning Sauce can be found in most conventional grocery stores, but you could easily substitute Worcestershire or a bit of soy sauce.

I want Gian Carlo to experience what I experienced when I was his age—the sights, sounds, smells, and fabulous flavors of Mexico.

—Chef Richard Sandoval

In Search of Avocados 15

*Modern Mexican Restaurants' philosophy is "old ways with new hands"—
I like to take traditional recipes from my grandmother in Mexico and
add my twist to them—that's where the modern comes in.*

—Chef Richard Sandoval

Chef Richard Sandoval
Black Bean Purée

PREPARATION

Place the black beans in a pot with the water. Add the onion, garlic, epazote, and salt. Cook over medium heat until tender, adding salt as desired. Let cool.

Purée until smooth, using a blender or similar device. Adjust the seasoning if needed.

The purée will keep for up to a week in the refrigerator. It is excellent as a dip for chips, tucked into a tortilla or burrito, alongside fish or meat, or as a topper to a salad.

INGREDIENTS

¾ cup black beans, *dry*
2 cups water
1 quartered piece of small onion
2 cloves garlic
5 epazote leaves
Salt, *to taste*

Chef Richard Sandoval
Chile de Arbol Sauce

PREPARATION

Slightly sauté the chile, onion, garlic, and tomato paste in the canola oil. Add the heavy cream and simmer until cooked, approximately 10 minutes. Add salt and pepper to taste. Remove from the heat. Let cool.

Pick through the cilantro, tearing it into small pieces. Add the cilantro pieces to the cooled sauce. Purée in a blender until smooth. Season to taste.

INGREDIENTS

1 tablespoon canola oil
2 pieces chile de arbol, *dried*
¼ small onion, *diced*
1 garlic clove
1 tablespoon tomato paste
¾ cup heavy cream
Salt and black pepper, *to taste*
2 tablespoons fresh cilantro

SOURCING NOTES

Epazote, pronounced "eh-paw-ZOH-teh," is well known in Mexican and Caribbean cooking. It is also known as pigweed or "Mexican tea." Epazote normally can be found in grocery stores, in both fresh and dried forms. One teaspoon of dried epazote leaves is equivalent to about 7 fresh leaves.

Chile de arbol is a long, red, slender, very hot chile pepper used in Mexican cooking. In Mexico, you'll also hear it called "bird's beak" or "rat's tail." The chile de arbol ranks 15,000–30,000 on the Scoville heat index—not quite as hot as the habanero chile. Look for dried chile de arbol in Latin markets, among the spices and chiles. If you prefer, you can substitute a milder chile of your liking.

KID-FRIENDLY COOKING

Washing and tearing herbs is perfect work for little hands. The smells, shapes, and tastes of the herbs are a perfect introduction to cooking for your young ones.

*In Mexico, we eat guacamole every day—
sometimes we add mangos, chipotles, or even lobster.*

—Chef Richard Sandoval

Chef Richard Sandoval
Guacamole de Gian Carlo

PREPARATION

Halve the avocados and remove the pits. Scoop the meat into a bowl and mash until *chunky*. Add the remaining ingredients and mix well. Taste, and adjust the seasoning with salt and lime.

ON THE PLATE

Serve with fresh or fried tortillas, atop fish or meat, or as a condiment.

YIELD ~ 4 PORTIONS

INGREDIENTS

2 large ripe Mexican Hass avocados, *halved*
¾ cup tomato, *small dice*
½ cup white onion, *small dice*
½ cup cilantro, *chopped*
½ serrano chile, *chopped*
Salt, *to taste*
Fresh lime juice, *to taste*

SOURCING NOTES

Hass is the most popular variety of avocado. Chef Sandoval prefers Hass because of its creamy, buttery texture and taste. Look for avocados that are marked as Hass avocados from Mexico for the very best consistency and taste.

When making guacamole, use avocados that are just becoming soft to the touch. For best quality, look for avocados with a dark, uniform skin color.

To ripen an avocado, place it on the counter or in front of a shaded window for a few days. If you need the avocado to ripen more quickly, simply wrap it in a paper bag or newspaper and place it at the back of the oven with the door closed and temperature off. Conversely, if you would like to stop an already "soft" avocado from ripening further, simply place it in the refrigerator until you are ready to use it.

KID-FRIENDLY COOKING

Guacamole is the perfect food for kids to work with. Let each child take a turn at mashing the avocados using a fork, the back of a spoon, or a potato masher. Let them sample along the way and adjust the taste to their liking.

Guacamole is a great, healthy alternative to butter on a sandwich, or it can be used as a topper to fish or meats.

In Search of Avocados

I want to play with your palate and senses to make eating more interactive and more fun.

I want to redefine what Americans think of as Mexican cuisine.

—Chef Richard Sandoval

Chef Richard Sandoval
Ceviche de Mahi Mahi

PREPARATION

Mix the lime juice and salt. Marinate the mahi mahi cubes in the lime mixture for up to 1 hour, in the refrigerator.

After marinating, strain the lime juice and discard any excess.

Combine the ingredients for the sauce: mix the ketchup, buffalo sauce, honey, and lemon juice and season to taste. Add the tomato, white onion, cilantro and serrano chile to the sauce.

Add the marinated and drained mahi mahi to sauce. Mix well.

ON THE PLATE

Serve in a cocktail glass or bowl (do not use metal bowl). Garnish with slices of fresh avocado and cilantro.

YIELD ~ 4 PORTIONS

INGREDIENTS

12 ounces mahi mahi filet, *cut into small cubes*
¾ cup lime juice, *freshly squeezed*
Salt, *to taste*
3 tablespoons ketchup
2 tablespoons "buffalo sauce"
1½ tablespoons honey
½ cup lemon juice
Salt, *to taste*
White ground pepper, *to taste*
1 cup tomato, *¼ inch dice*
½ cup onion, *¼ inch dice*
3 tablespoons cilantro, *chopped*
½ serrano chile, *chopped, to taste*
Avocado slices, *for garnish*
Cilantro, *for garnish*

SOURCING NOTES

"Buffalo Sauce" is a common ingredient in Mexican cooking and usually can be found in Latin markets. The sauce is both sweet and spicy. As a substitute, use your favorite hot sauce.

You can substitute a variety of fish for the mahi mahi in this recipe; shrimp, scallops, and halibut are all good choices. The freshest, best seafood is required, however. Ask your fishmonger for "sashimi grade."

Many of the world's marine species are dangerously over-fished and in decline. Still others are considered polluted and unsafe for recipes such as this. Whenever possible, consult a sustainable seafood guide like the one available at SEAFOODCHOICES.ORG.

KID-FRIENDLY COOKING

This recipe is not only simple but easy for the kids to get involved with. Let the kids use scissors to cut the fish into small pieces and their might to squeeze the lemons and limes. And, of course, allow them to taste along the way.

Have the kids create their own unique presentations. Let them choose from various glasses or bowls. Use avocado, onion, tomato slices, mango, crab, cilantro or other herbs for decoration, if they like. Or, help them place ceviche in a "bowl" of lettuce or cabbage. Allow the kids to experiment and create their own presentation.

GROW "GREEN GOLD" ~
SPROUT YOUR OWN AVOCADO PLANT

In Mexico, they call the avocado "green gold" because of its great value. Its characteristic flavor, creamy texture, and taste have made it the favorite of chefs around the world. The volcanic soil of Mexico's Michoacán region makes it the ideal place to grow avocados. Ninety percent of the world's avocados come from Mexico.

It's easy to grow your own avocado plant from a seed. Keep the plant indoors unless you live in a warm climate with rich soil. Be patient; it takes approximately five years for a new plant to bear fruit.

WHAT YOU NEED
- Ripe avocado
- Knife
- Three round, wooden toothpicks
- Drinking glass
- Water

WHAT YOU DO
- Cut the avocado in half, being careful not to cut into the seed.
- Remove the seed and wash it in warm water to remove any pulp and the brown covering.
- With the pointed side of the seed up, insert the toothpicks, evenly spaced, into the seed.
- Suspend the seed (broad end down) over a water-filled glass. The water should cover an inch of the seed at all times.
- Put the glass in a warm place, but not in direct sunlight. In two to six weeks, the seed will crack as roots, stem, and leaves sprout.
- When the roots are thick and the stem has leafed out, plant the seedling in a pot with potting soil, leaving half of the seed exposed.
- Water your avocado thoroughly, but allow it to dry out between waterings.

NATURAL GAS ~ READY & RIPE

- To find out whether an avocado is ripe, press gently on the bottom with your thumb. If it's slightly soft, it's ripe and ready to eat. To ripen an avocado in a day or two, simply place the fruit in a paper bag and fold over the top. Keep the avocado dry and at room temperature.

What goes on inside the bag? An avocado releases ethylene gas that stimulates the ripening process. The bag speeds ripening because it traps ethylene gas and concentrates it around the avocado.

ALL GROWN UP ~ SEED SEARCH

While preparing the *Piramide de Res* recipe from Chef Sandoval, find—and compare—the seeds in each of these ingredients:

- Lemon
- Avocado
- Chile peppers
- Lime
- Black bean
- Garlic
- Tomato
- Onion
- Bell Pepper

- Which has the largest seeds? Which has the smallest? Which has the most seeds? Which has the fewest? Which one of these is itself a seed? Which are similar?

These seeds may differ in size, shape, and color, but each does the same job. Each contains an embryo—the beginning of a new plant.

Seeds also contain varying amounts of stored food to nourish the embryo until leaves form and the plant can begin to make food through photosynthesis. We eat seeds, such as beans and nuts, because the embryonic plant and stored food are nutritious.

FACTOID ~ DID YOU KNOW?

Avocados probably originated in Mexico more than twelve thousand years ago. Before the arrival of Europeans, avocados were cultivated on land ranging from south of the Rio Grande to Peru. These luscious fruits were an important part of the diet of indigenous people, including the Aztecs and Mayas.

The superior quality of the Hass variety of avocados grown in Michoacán, Mexico, can be attributed to the region's rich volcanic soil, warm sun, varying altitudes, and the fact that it receives just the right amount of rainfall. All of these things create an ideal microclimate for developing the fruit's superior flavor and texture.

VARIETY IS THE SPICE OF LIFE ~
THE OLD WORLD MEETS THE NEW WORLD

Today we are used to eating fruits and vegetables that have been grown around the world and that are available in our stores throughout the year. But before Columbus' voyages from Europe to the Americas, there was no chocolate in Switzerland or tomato sauce in Italy because cacao beans and tomatoes grew only in the New World. Likewise, there was no orange juice or pasta in the New World because oranges and wheat grew only in the Old World.

※ **CREATE THREE DISHES:** one that uses only New World ingredients such as avocado and tomato, a second with only Old World ingredients such as lentils and spinach, and a third with both New and Old World ingredients such as pumpkin and wheat flour.

NEW WORLD CROPS	OLD WORLD CROPS	
avocados	almonds	olives
beans	apple	onions
bell peppers	apricots	peaches
blueberries	aparagus	pears
cashew nuts	bananas	radishes
corn	barley	rice
chile peppers	beets	spinach
cacao beans	blackberries	sugar cane
green beans	carrots	turnips
papaya	cauliflower	walnuts
pecans	celery	wheat
peanuts	cherries	yams
pineapples	chick peas	
potatoes	coffee	
strawberries	citrus fruits	
squash	cucumbers	
sugar maple	dates	
sunflowers	eggplants	
sweet potatoes	figs	
tomatoes	garlic	
vanilla	lettuces	

ROUGHING IT ~ FIBER IS YOUR FRIEND

You have probably heard that eating foods rich in fiber is good for you. But what is dietary fiber? It's the part of a food plant that your body can't digest or absorb. Fruits, vegetables, and whole grains are high in fiber. Fiber is best known for helping to prevent constipation. But it also can help lower cholesterol, reduce the risk of diabetes, and aid in weight control.

Adults need to eat 20 to 35 grams of fiber each day (although the average consumption is about half that amount), and children older than two require an amount equal to their age in years, plus 5 grams, every day.

※ Here are some of the ingredients in Chef Sandoval's *Piramide de Res* recipe, with the amount of dietary fiber contained in a typical serving of each. Rank them in order from highest to lowest fiber content.

FOOD	PORTION	GRAMS OF FIBER
White onion	1 slice	0.2
Skirt steak	4 ounces	0.0
Black Bean Puree	½ cup	7.5
Avocado	4 ounces	7.6
Corn tortilla chips	1 ounce	1.5
Garlic	1 clove	0.1
Chopped tomato	½ cup	1.3

ACTIVITIES

chefsafield.com

Walnut Shaking

featuring

CHEF MICHAEL MINA
MICHAEL MINA RESTAURANTS
MICHAEL MINA SAN FRANCISCO / LAS VEGAS
ARCADIA SAN JOSE, CALIFORNIA
STONEHILL TAVERN DANA POINT, CALIFORNIA
NOBHILL LAS VEGAS, NEVADA
SEABLUE LAS VEGAS / ATLANTIC CITY
STRIPSTEAK LAS VEGAS, NEVADA

BILL CARRIERE
CARRIERE & SONS GLENN, CALIFORNIA

Michael Mina is considered by many to be one of the world's very best chefs. At the center of his cooking are impeccable ingredients gathered from farmers he trusts.

In this culinary adventure, Chef Mina and his two sons, Sammy, age eight, and Anthony, age four, head to the Sacramento Valley, where the walnuts are ripe and ready for the picking. But picking isn't exactly how they harvest a tree exploding with nuts.

Instead, the boys climb into a giant Tonka®-like truck from which they literally shake the tree branches—using long pinchers attached to mechanical arms.

The earth rumbles and a fireworks display of walnuts comes raining down, to the delight of the excited children below.

Fourth-generation farmer Bill Carriere and his three children lead the way as the Minas follow along, eating, tasting, and learning about the walnut.

*It is hard work, but it's worth it.
We have a great life out here.*

–Bill Carriere

Great food starts with the farmers— farming that is done right.
—Chef Michael Mina

Walnut Shaking

Chef Michael Mina
Blue Cheese & Walnut Soufflés

INGREDIENTS

1½ cups milk
4 tablespoons (½ stick) unsalted butter
1½ cups all-purpose flour
6 large farm-fresh eggs, *yolks only*
8 ounces Roquefort cheese
2 tablespoons chives, *minced*
1 teaspoon black pepper
2 cups farm-fresh eggs, *whites only*
1 teaspoon cream of tartar

PREPARATION

To make the pâte à choux, which is the base of the soufflé, bring the milk and butter to a gentle boil over medium heat in a heavy-bottomed saucepan. When the butter is completely melted, add the flour. Reduce heat to low and stir vigorously until the dough pulls away from the sides of the pan, about 3 to 5 minutes. The dough should not stick to your hands when pressed.

Scrape the dough into the bowl of a standing electric mixer. With the paddle attachment, mix the dough on medium-low speed until cool. Once the dough is cool, add the egg yolks, one at a time, stopping to scrape down the sides of the bowl periodically. The dough should be sticky and bright yellow. (The pâte à choux may be prepared to this point a day in advance, then covered and refrigerated, or it can be frozen for up to a month.)

Add the blue cheese, chives, and pepper into the mixer. Mix until consistent. Place the egg whites and cream of tartar in a clean mixer bowl. Fit the machine with the whisk attachment and turn to low. Beat the egg whites on low until very frothy. Turn the mixer to high and whisk until medium peaks have formed.
Gently fold the egg whites into the blue-cheese mixture in 3 or 4 additions, being careful to avoid deflating the whites. Once all of the whites have been incorporated, place the mixture in the refrigerator.

Generously butter and flour 6 8-ounce ramekins. Use a large ice-cream scoop to fill the ramekins with the mixture. Place the ramekins on a baking sheet and into a preheated 350° F oven for 12 to 15 minutes. When done, the soufflés should be golden brown and light to the touch.

ON THE PLATE
Pierce the tops of the soufflés slightly and pour a generous portion of Toasted Walnut Cream on top of each. *(See accompanying recipe.)* If desired, top with Blue Cheese & Watercress Salad. *(See accompanying recipe.)* Serve immediately.

YIELD ~ 6 APPETIZER PORTIONS

I fell in love with cooking because I love making people happy.

-Chef Michael Mina

SOURCING NOTES
Using farm-fresh eggs will make the soufflés especially fluffy and rich. Farm-fresh eggs from pasture-raised chickens have a thicker consistency than conventional eggs. Their yolks are brighter yellow and the whites tend to whip higher. Look for locally produced eggs at your market or grocer. Many specialty stores now sell fresh, locally produced eggs labeled from their farms of origin.

KID-FRIENDLY COOKING
This soufflé is not only elegant, but particularly easy to make with children, as the pâte à choux technique makes it nearly foolproof. Let the kids whip the egg whites by hand with a whisk. They will be especially delighted to see the rising soufflés fresh from the oven.

Chef Michael Mina
Blue Cheese & Watercress Salad with Walnut Vinaigrette

INGREDIENTS
¼ cup champagne vinegar
¼ cup toasted walnut oil
½ cup canola oil
Salt and pepper, *to taste*
4 bunches watercress, *washed, stems removed*
1 Bosc pear, *sliced thin*
4 ounces Roquefort cheese, *crumbled*
½ cup walnut halves, *toasted*

PREPARATION
Whisk the vinegar, walnut oil, canola, oil and salt together in a small bowl. Set aside. Season the watercress with salt and pepper, and drizzle the desired amount of dressing on top. Toss the salad well.

ON THE PLATE
Arrange the sliced pear, blue cheese, and toasted walnut halves on your serving plates. Divide the watercress among the plates, placing atop the pear slices, cheese, and walnut halves. Top with additional cheese if desired.

YIELD ~ 4 SERVINGS

KID-FRIENDLY COOKING
When it comes time to make the vinaigrette, place all the ingredients in a small jar. Let the kids add the measured ingredients, then tightly close the jar. Let them take turns shaking the jar and watching the ingredients emulsify.

Making dressings are also a wonderful way to farmiliarize kids with their taste senses and particularly, with the various flavors of herbs. Place verious herbs, oils, salts, and other acidic components (such as lemons and vinegar) out on a platter and let each child experiment with inventing their own flavor of vinaigrette.

Chef Michael Mina
Toasted Walnut Cream

PREPARATION

Place the shallots, wine, walnuts, and thyme into a sauce pot over low heat. Simmer until most of the wine has reduced. Add the cream to the pot and allow it to steep for 20 minutes over low heat. The sauce will thicken slightly and should pick up the walnut flavor. Strain the sauce, and season to taste.

ON THE PLATE

Serve warm as an accompaniment to Blue Cheese & Walnut Soufflés. *(See accompanying recipe.)*

This cream also makes an excellent accompaniment to fish, chicken, or even seasonal vegetables such as cauliflower, broccoli, or greens.

INGREDIENTS

2 shallots, *sliced*

1 cup dry white wine

1 cup toasted California walnuts, *shelled*

2 sprigs fresh thyme

2 cups heavy cream

Salt and pepper, *to taste*

Chef Michael Mina
Caramelized Walnut & Fruit Tart Tatin

INGREDIENTS

FOR THE CARAMEL
- ¾ cup sugar
- 2 tablespoons water
- 2 tablespoons unsalted butter, cut into chunks

FOR THE TART
- 2 cups fresh fruit, berries, or bananas *use whatever is in season in your area
- 1 frozen puff pastry sheet, *thawed*
- 1½ cups fresh California walnuts, toasted and chopped
- ½ cup powdered sugar
- 1 tablespoon cinnamon
- 1 large farm-fresh egg
- 1 tablespoon water

PREPARATION

FOR THE CARAMEL:
Combine the sugar and 2 tablespoons water in a 10-inch ovenproof sauté pan. Cook over medium heat without stirring until the sugar melts and begins to caramelize into syrup, about 3 minutes. Once the sugar starts to liquefy, stir with a wooden spoon to keep it from burning.

Continue to cook until the sugar begins to boil and takes on a medium-amber color, about 2 minutes more. Watch out—the sugar is very hot. Remove from the heat and stir in the butter to melt, along with half of the walnuts. Set the pan aside so the caramel firms up slightly.

FOR THE TART:
Preheat the oven to 475° F. Pick your favorite fruit: bananas, strawberries, blueberries, or other seasonal fruit. Wash, dry, and prepare the fruit. If using any fruit larger than a blueberry, slice it into coin-sized pieces.

Combine the powdered sugar and cinnamon. Generously sprinkle the sugar mixture on a work surface. Lay the puff pastry sheet over the sugar mixture. Sprinkle the pastry with the remaining chopped walnuts and a generous sprinkling of cinnamon sugar. Flatten the pastry with a rolling pin, pressing the walnuts into the pastry. Set a dinner plate on top of the pastry and cut around the outside rim to make a 10-inch circle. (If making individual tarts, use a saucer or smaller mold as your guide.)

Pour the reserved caramel into tart pan(s), just covering the bottom. Place the fruit on top of the caramel coating, filling the tart pan(s). Cover the fruit with a disk of puff pastry. Make 3 small slits in the top of the pastry, to let the steam escape. Beat the egg and 1 tablespoon water together to make an egg wash. Brush the top of each tart with egg wash.

Bake 30 minutes for one large tart or 12 minutes for small tarts. Bake until the pastry is puffed and golden while the filling is bubbly. Remove from oven. Let the tart rest for 1 minute. Run a knife around the inside rim of the pan to make sure the tart will come out easily. Set a serving plate face down on top of the pan and quickly flip the pan over to invert the tart.

ON THE PLATE
Cut the tart into wedges. Top each serving with a generous scoop of Brown Sugar & Walnut Ice Cream.

YIELD ~ 1 (8 ½-INCH) TART, OR CAN BE DIVIDED INTO 8 INDIVIDUAL TARTS

Walnut Shaking 33

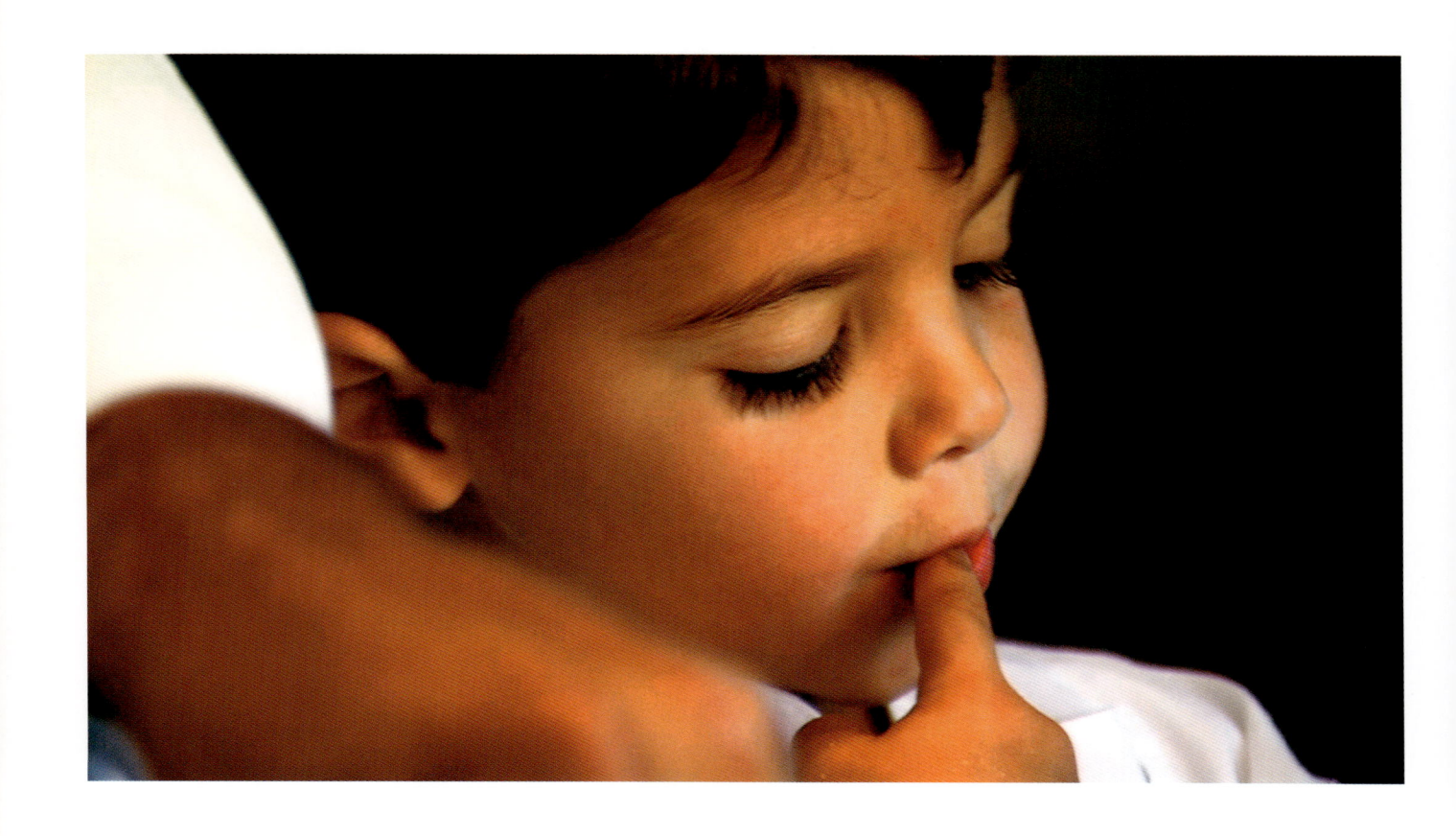

The great thing about cooking with your kids is that it is something they are going to take with them and use for the rest of their lives. ... It is a life skill, so why not learn how to do it at an early age?

–Chef Michael Mina

Chef Michael Mina
"Anthony's Favorite" Brown Sugar & Walnut Ice Cream

PREPARATION

Combine the cream, milk, sugar, and salt in a large pot. Place the pot over medium heat. Bring to a simmer while stirring to dissolve the sugar.

Once the sugar has dissolved, add the toasted walnuts and allow them to steep. Ideally the temperature should reach 175° F (just below scalding); this should take about 5 minutes.

In a large mixing bowl, whisk the egg yolks until thick. Using a large ladle, *temper* the yolks by gradually whisking half of the hot cream mixture into the yolk mixture. Do not add it too quickly, or the eggs will cook and begin to scramble.

Add the tempered egg yolks into the pot and whisk constantly over medium heat until the custard is thick enough to coat the back of a spoon. This takes about 5 minutes.

Pass the custard through a fine-mesh strainer into a large container. Chill the container completely by placing it in a large bowl full of ice water, stirring the custard occasionally. This should take between 5 and 10 minutes.

Churn the custard in an ice-cream maker according to the manufacturer's directions. When done, the ice cream will be the consistency of soft-serve. To harden the ice cream fully, freeze it in a covered plastic container.

YIELD ~ 1 QUART

INGREDIENTS

3¼ cups heavy cream
1¼ cups milk
1 cup brown sugar
½ teaspoon salt
1 cup California walnuts, *toasted*
11 large farm-fresh eggs, *yolks only*
1 teaspoon natural vanilla extract

SOURCING NOTES

Using good, quality sugar makes a big difference in recipes such as the Walnut Ice Cream. There are many natural and organic sugars to choose from these days. Try experimenting to find a flavor that the whole family likes, from Sucanat to Demarrera to Cane or even Agave. A favorite source of ours is Wholesome Sweeteners orgnic sugars. Find them at your local Whole Foods Market or online at WHOLESOMESWEETENERS.COM

KID-FRIENDLY COOKING

Chef Mina's Ice Cream and Fruit Tartin recipes are sure to become a household favorite with the kids, not only for the taste, but for how much fun they are to make. From crushing (or chopping) the walnuts by hand and filling the cups with their favorite fruit, to rolling the pin to flatten the pastry, to whisking the eggs and watching the ice cream harden, these allow kids of all ages to get involved.

'BUTTER ME UP ~ MAKING WALNUT BUTTER

Because nuts and seeds have a high oil content, they can be ground into buttery spreads.

Peanut butter is perhaps the most familiar to Americans, but there are many "nutty butters." Roasted sesame seeds are ground into tahini, a common ingredient in Middle Eastern recipes. Almonds are ground with sugar to make marzipan, or almond paste, which is used in making candies and cake decorations throughout Europe.

Walnuts can make a particularly healthful "butter" because their oil is high in omega-3 fatty acids, which may help reduce the risk of heart disease, stroke, and cancer.

The walnut is the only nut that contains a significant amount of omega-3 fatty acids.

WHAT YOU NEED
- 2 cups shelled walnuts
- Cookie sheet
- 1 tablespoon vegetable oil
- Blender or food processor

WHAT YOU DO
- Preheat the oven to 350°F.
- Spread the walnuts on a cookie sheet and roast for 8 to 10 minutes until they are browned, but not burned (check frequently.)
- In a blender or food processor, pureé the roasted walnuts with the vegetable oil, until smooth.
- Store in a sealed container and refrigerate.

Raw and roasted nuts taste different. Compare the taste of a walnut you have roasted with one you have not. Which do you prefer? What are the similarities and differences?

LET'S PLAY! ~ WALNUT PLAY DOUGH

Who doesn't love to play with their food? Now that you have made Walnut Butter, you can either spread it on some toast—or you can use it to make your own, edible play dough.

WHAT YOU NEED
- 1 cup walnut butter
- 1 cup powdered milk
- 1 tablespoon honey

WHAT YOU DO
- Mix all of the ingredients together with your hands, kneading it until thoroughly mixed.

Use your play dough to create fun shapes. The best part is that you can eat your creations when you are done—no cooking is required!

Dough can be stored in the refrigerator in an air-tight container for up to 1 week.

TO SHELL OR NOT TO SHELL ~
NUTS ABOUT MATH

For a recipe, you need 4 ounces of shelled walnuts. How many ounces of whole walnuts do you need?

HERE'S HOW TO FIND OUT
- Gather 10 walnuts in the shell. Weigh them. Crack them open and separate the shells from the meat. But don't eat any yet!
- Weigh the shells and nut meat separately. Record your results.
- You should find that the nuts and shells weigh just about the same. The walnuts' weight is divided almost exactly in half between nut and shell.
- So in your recipe, you will need 8 ounces of walnuts in the shell to equal 4 ounces of shelled walnut meat.

PRICE PREDICTIONS ~
WHICH COSTS MORE:
BUYING WALNUTS IN THE SHELL . . .
OR BUYING WALNUTS SHELLED?

- To figure out which costs more, go to the store. Find a bag of shelled walnuts and one of unshelled walnuts.
- Do the math to find out the cost per ounce of each bag. Remember, the bag containing the unshelled walnuts is about half full of shell and half full of walnut meat.
- Which is the better buy, ounce for ounce? Walnut for walnut?

FACTOID ~
WHO FIRST ATE A WALNUT?
Probably a smart woman—a "gatherer" in pursuit of nourishing food—in Persia about 8,000 years ago. Walnut trees first grew in Persia, which is the area now occupied by Iran.

ARE YOU NUTS? ~
WALNUTS AROUND THE WORLD
If laid end-to-end, how many walnuts (in the shell) would it take to circle the Equator?

- The average California walnut in the shell is 1½ inches across.
- The equator is 24,901 miles around.
- One mile is 5,280 feet.

Answer: 1,051,818,240 walnuts

How many walnuts would it take to go from the Earth to the moon?

HINT: The moon is 222,756 miles from the Earth.

Answer: 9,409,213,440 walnuts

TRICK OR TREAT? ~ THE MAGIC SHELL GAME
The shell game has been played at least since the Middle Ages. It can be played honestly or as a trick—so be sure you have a trustworthy partner!

TO PLAY:
You need three walnut shell halves, as alike in size and color as possible. Line up the three shells on a table. Put a walnut piece (or dried bean) under one shell. Shuffle the shells around the table as fast as you can, ending with the three shells back in one line. Can you identify where the walnut piece is? If you guess right, you get to eat the walnut piece as your prize!

The shell game often was played by gamblers who would bet on where they thought the bean was. The game often was turned into a swindle, however, by fast-fingered operators who moved the bean so it was never under the shell that the player had selected.

ACTIVITIES

I love growing something that people really enjoy ...
and I love growing something that is healthy and good for you.

-BILL CARRIERE

Chesapeake Rockfish Roundup

featuring

CHEF ROBERT WIEDMAIER
MARCEL'S WASHINGTON, D.C.
BRASSERIE BECK WASHINGTON, D.C.

JIM CHAMBERS
PRIME SEAFOOD KENSINGTON, MARYLAND

The rockfish, known by most as the striped bass, was virtually extinct 15 years ago, when many felt the Chesapeake Bay could no longer sustain its ecosystem.

Today, the rockfish is an environmental success story, and the bay is now in recovery.

Chef Robert Wiedmaier began his culinary career at sea, cooking for researchers aboard a vessel protesting over-fishing and whaling. Today, Chef Wiedmaier is one of Washington, D.C.'s most acclaimed chefs, with two restaurants, each named for one of his sons.

In this culinary adventure, Chef Wiedmaier and his two sons, Beck, age three, and Marcel, age seven, along with their seven-year-old friend Lars, haul in a healthy catch as they spend the day on the Chesapeake Bay, rounding up rockfish.

As they catch and release the bass, marine biologist Jim Chambers is on hand to explain the bay's ecosystem and describe what makes the rockfish recovery so special. And of course, no story is complete without a few "big ones," caught by the young fishermen to take home for dinner.

Chef Robert Wiedmaier
Chesapeake Rockfish with Sunburst Squash & Chive-Tomato Beurre Blanc

INGREDIENTS

FOR THE ROCKFISH
- 2 filets of rockfish, *or wild striped bass*
- 1 small bunch fresh thyme sprigs
- 1 clove garlic, *smashed*
- Salt and pepper, *to taste*

FOR THE SQUASH
- 1 tablespoon butter
- 3 small sunburst squash, *quartered*
- 1 handful shiitake mushrooms, *quartered*
- 3 medium shallots, *chopped*

FOR THE BEURRE BLANC
- 4 tablespoons butter
- ¼ cup shallots, *sliced*
- 4–5 sprigs fresh thyme
- ½ cup vermouth
- ¼ cup heavy cream
- 1 tomato, *small dice*
- 1 small bunch chives, *chopped*

PREPARATION

FOR THE ROCKFISH:
Wash and pat dry the rockfish filets. Season the fish with salt and pepper.

FOR THE BEURRE BLANC:
Place a sauté pan over medium-high heat. Add 2 tablespoons of the butter, ¼ cup sliced shallots, and 4–5 sprigs fresh thyme. *Sweat* the shallots and thyme until tender and translucent, about 5 minutes. Add the vermouth to the mixture and boil until the liquid is reduced by ¾. Remove from the heat. Slowly pour in the heavy cream. Rapidly whisk in the remaining butter. Add the diced tomato and the chives. Gently stir to incorporate.

FOR THE SQUASH:
Heat a sauté pan over medium heat. Melt 1 tablespoon butter in the pan. Sauté the squash, mushrooms, and 3 medium shallots in the butter until tender, about 5 minutes.

Meanwhile, heat a grill or sauté pan until very hot. Remove the skin from the rockfish, if desired. Remove the pan from the stove and carefully place the rockfish in it. Cook on medium-high heat for approximately 2 minutes or until the fish begins turning opaque. Flip the fish, and add the small bunch of thyme sprigs and the garlic to the pan. Continue cooking until achieving desired doneness, cooking for approximately 3 more minutes for medium-rare. Remove the fish from the heat and let it rest.

ON THE PLATE
Place the warm squash-and-mushroom mixture on the plate. Place the warm fish on top of the vegetables. Generously scoop the sauce atop and along the sides of the fish.

YIELD ~ 2 SERVINGS

SOURCING NOTES
When purchasing rockfish, or striped bass, look for species that are line-caught. Some trawling techniques have negative impacts on the seafloor, causing long-term environmental damage to ecosystems and plant life. Populations of rockfish and striped bass are particularly abundant and thriving in the Chesapeake, Cape Cod, and Alaska, where fisheries management has helped the fish rebound.

Many areas of the United States have unique varieties of squash, as well as locally harvested or foraged mushrooms. Use whatever varieties are available and fresh at your local market.

We have to be conscious of what fish species we catch and eat so future generations can enjoy the same seafood we love today.

–Chef Robert Wiedmaier

Chesapeake Rockfish Roundup 41

Chef Robert Wiedmaier
Roasted Red Snapper with Melon & Citrus Emulsion

INGREDIENTS

FOR THE SNAPPER

2 filets of red snapper, *cleaned and with skin left on*
1 teaspoon olive oil
1 small bunch fresh thyme sprigs
2 cloves garlic, *slightly smashed*
Salt and pepper, *to taste*

FOR THE EMULSION

½ cup fresh watermelon
½ cup fresh cantaloupe
½ cup fresh honeydew melon
2 cups orange juice
½ cup honey
½ cup balsamic vinegar
4 cups canola oil
2 tablespoons cilantro, *chopped*

PREPARATION

Use the smallest melon scoop available to form balls from each melon. Combine all of the melon balls in a bowl. Set aside.

Place the orange juice in a saucepan over high heat. Boil until reduced to approximately ½ cup. Set the reduced orange juice aside or in the refrigerator to cool.

Combine the honey, vinegar, and orange juice in a blender. Slowly add the canola oil to emulsify.

Heat a dry cast-iron or sauté pan (large enough to hold the snapper filets) over high heat. While the pan heats, season the snapper with salt and pepper. Once it's hot, carefully remove the pan from the heat. Add the olive oil to the pan and gently lay the snapper in it, skin-side down. Cook for about 3 minutes. Turn the fish. Toss the thyme sprigs and garlic atop the fish. Baste with oil and any juices that have accumulated in the pan. Continue to cook for approximately 3 minutes more. Remove from the heat and let the fish rest.

Meanwhile, add the melon balls and cilantro to the orange juice emulsion. Stir to coat the melon.

ON THE PLATE

Place a generous scoop of the melon mixture on the plate. Place the fish atop the melon mélange. Drizzle additional spoonfuls of the melon-and-orange juice emulsion atop the fish. Place garlic and thyme sprigs from the sauté pan alongside or atop the fish for decoration. Serve warm.

YIELD ~ 4 SERVINGS

KID-FRIENDLY COOKING

Let the kids help choose the melons for this recipe by taking them along to your local farmers market. Many melons have fun names: "Moon and Stars," "Popsicle Pink," "Tangerine Melon," "Sunrise Surprise," "Green Dream." At most markets, the farmers will let you sample the wide variety of flavors available.

When you get the melons home, let the kids be responsible for scooping them into balls or other fun shapes. Slice the melons into flat pieces for the children. Then let them use extra-small cookie cutters or teaspoons to create their own unique designs.

When buying seafood, a fresh fish should never smell "fishy," its gills should be bright red, its eyes clear and not cloudy. If a fish is bad, it's going to tell you just by looking at it.

—Chef Robert Wieidmaier

Chesapeake Rockfish Roundup

FISH FACTS ~ GET A BACKBONE!
People and fish are vertebrates: They both have backbones.

✳ Take a trip to the fish store or fish department of your supermarket to discover which other parts of the body fish and people share, and which ones they don't.

Arms	Legs	Backbone
Fins	Scales	Teeth
Hair	Eyes	Tongue
Lungs	Gills	Tail
Mouth	Blood	Ribs

It's important to protect our environment. Everything we do on land affects our marine ecosystem …

—Chef Robert Wiedmaier

HANDS OFF ~ THE GREAT ROCKFISH COMEBACK!
In the 1970s and 1980s, Atlantic rockfish (striped bass) were in trouble. Their population in the Chesapeake Bay tumbled because of overfishing and pollution.

The fishing industry imposed severe limits on the size and number of rockfish that could be caught. After more than a decade of restrictions, the population bounced back. Now, striped bass and rockfish are at record levels in many parts of the United States, making them an "eco-friendly" choice to buy.

Eco-friendly seafood is also "sustainable," which means that it is fished or farmed in ways that don't jeopardize either the fish population or its ecosystem. Some of the issues related to the seafood industry are:

✳ **BYCATCH:** Unwanted fish and other animals, such as birds and turtles, are accidentally caught in nets and then discarded, often dying in the process. New technologies and good management can help reduce bycatch and limit injuries.

✳ **HABITAT DAMAGE:** Wetlands, where fish breed, have been paved over or polluted. Parts of the seafloor where some fish live are torn up by trawlers and dredges. Fishing with hook and line is preferable to trawling.

✳ **AQUACULTURE (FISH FARMING):** Fish farms can pollute the water with the waste products of thousands of fish concentrated in a small area. Escaped fish can spread disease or outnumber wild fish in the area. Moving fish farms inland is a sustainable alternative to coastal farming.

✳ **OVER-FISHING:** When fish are caught faster than they can reproduce, populations rapidly decline. International cooperation to manage fish catches is needed to keep fish populations at sustainable levels.

You can get a list of sustainable, eco-friendly seafood choices—and find out what you can do to ensure that our fish species stay healthy—by visiting one of these Web sites:

MONTEREYBAYAQUARIUM.ORG   SEAFOODCHOICES.COM   BLUEOCEAN.ORG

FACTOID ~ DID YOU KNOW?
In the Chesapeake Bay, "rockfish" is another name for striped bass, *morone saxatilis*. It is thought that the name "rockfish" came from early settlers who found the fish congregating around rocks.

DOWN THE DRAIN ~
SUSTAINABILITY STARTS IN YOUR BACKYARD
Water pollution severely threatens fish populations around the world.

Even if you don't live near a body of water, you can help keep pollutants out of the water in which fish live. That's because wherever you live, you live in a watershed—the land area that drains water into a stream, river, lake, bay, or ocean.

Water, whether it comes from rain, snow, or a garden hose, crosses forests, farms, lawns, and city streets and can pick up pollutants on the way. Pollutants can wipe out fish populations very quickly and even poison us when we eat fish that swim in polluted waters.

※ Look around your neighborhood. What are some of the ways that you and your neighbors can help keep pollutants out of our water and away from fish?

- **MOTOR OIL & ANTIFREEZE** can damage or kill underwater plants and animals. NEVER pour used motor oil or antifreeze down a storm drain, onto the soil, or into a waterway. Put used oil or antifreeze in a sturdy container and take it to a local service station or other approved center that will dispose of it properly.
- **OIL & ANTIFREEZE** that leak out of cars can wash into storm drains when it rains. Check your cars for drips and leaks. If you find any, have them fixed soon!
- **TO REDUCE RUNOFF,** place sprinklers so that the water goes only on the lawn instead of watering the street or sidewalk. This will keep any pollutants or fertilizers on your lawn from running down the street and into the watershed.
- **STREET LITTER,** such as plastic bags, cups, and candy wrappers, often gets swept away with rainwater into storm drains. Eventually, the litter can end up floating in the ocean or washing up on beaches. There marine animals can mistake plastics for food or can become tangled up in them. Recycle as much of your trash as possible, and put all other litter in garbage cans.
- **LEAVE MOWED GRASS CLIPPINGS ON THE LAWN.** They are a good source of nutrients for the grass, hence reducing the need for fertilizers. Clippings also reduce erosion. If you remove grass clippings, you can compost them with fallen leaves.
- **FERTILIZERS** contain large amounts of nutrients such as nitrogen and phosphorous that can wash into lakes and streams. These nutrients may cause algal blooms that can smother other aquatic life. Pesticides and herbicides also contain toxic materials that can run off into storm drains and nearby waterways. Eliminate fertilizers and pesticides from your routine. Instead, incorporate organic and natural methods. Visit your local garden store and ask for organic products that are safe for you and the environment.

PLEASE PASS THE SALT ~ CHANGING TASTES
Cooks know that a little salt can make bitter things taste less bitter and sweet things taste sweeter.

※ Select several foods and set up a blind tasting. You could include, for example, unsweetened cocoa powder (not Dutch processed), black coffee, radish, watermelon, and grapefruit. Taste them as they are and then with a few grains of salt added. How does the taste change?

FACTOID ~ HARD ROCK
DID YOU KNOW...
Salt is the only mineral that we eat.
Sea salt comes from dehydrated sea water.

ACTIVITIES

California Strawberries

featuring

CHEFS MITCHELL & STEVEN ROSENTHAL
TOWN HALL RESTAURANT SAN FRANCISCO, CALIFORNIA

VICTOR RAMIREZ
STRAWBERRY GROWER WATSONVILLE, CALIFORNIA

The California strawberry is the star of this culinary adventure above the misty shores of Monterey Bay. The Pacific breezes and warm California sun nurture a berry so sweet that it is the choice of chefs from around the world.

Great cooking runs in the family at San Francisco's Town Hall Restaurant, as brothers and fellow chefs Mitchell and Steven Rosenthal show their kids how to cook sweet and savory dishes with the juicy California strawberry.

But first, they gather the berries. Chef Mitchell and kids meet farmer Victor Ramirez and his daughters. The children happily pick—and eat—their way through the berry rows together, filling box upon box with delicious strawberries.

The kids also get a lesson in entomology and botany. Farmer Ramirez shows how a flower becomes fruit, and the "bug detective" is on hand with a microscope to offer the children a closer look at the difference between "good bugs" and "bad bugs."

The berry-stained kids head back to Town Hall Restaurant, where Uncle Steven gets everyone in on the cooking, baking, and tasting.

Chefs Mitchell and Steven Rosenthal
Homemade California Strawberry Jam Preserves

INGREDIENTS
2 pounds fresh strawberries, *hulled and halved*
3 cups sugar
½ lemon, *juiced*
6 ounces liquid pectin

SOURCING NOTES
Pectin is a naturally occurring acidic fiber found in berries and other fruits. Your grandmother probably made pectin by boiling and boiling and boiling berries or fruit skins into thick syrup. The proteins that break down make up the pectin of the fruit. It is commonly used as a thickener in cooking. Find all-natural versions of pectin in foil packets at your local grocer.

KID-FRIENDLY COOKING
This recipe is virtually foolproof, making it a good choice for cooking with the kids. Let the kids help you pull the green tops off of the berries, help pour the sugar, and mix the berries during the maceration stage. And, of course, let them taste along the way.

Visit a local berry farm for some summer fun. Strawberries grow at just the right height for the little ones—and there are never any thorns to sting small hands. Or try growing your own in a container on the deck.

PREPARATION
Toss the strawberries with 1 cup of the sugar and leave to macerate until the juices are released: about 1 hour, or up to 8 hours. Put the remaining sugar in a shallow pan and place in a 200° F oven to keep warm.

Place the macerated strawberries and their liquid in a large saucepan. Add the lemon juice. Gently warm the contents of the pan and add the warmed sugar. Stir gently until all the sugar has dissolved.

Raise the heat and boil the liquid vigorously until foam appears on the surface. Using a spoon, skim off the foam. Stir in the pectin and boil until the desired consistency is reached, about 5 to 10 minutes.

You can check the consistency of the jam by placing a spoonful on a chilled plate. When the jam is the desired consistency, remove the saucepan from the heat.

Once you've removed the pan from the heat, skim any remaining foam from the surface and let stand 10 to 15 minutes.

IF CANNING OR STORING FOR LATER:
Sterilize clean jars and lids in boiling water; invert onto paper towels, and leave to airdry. When the jam is cooled, pour it into the sterile jars, being sure not to fill them more than ¾ full.

Seal the lids tightly and submerge the jars in a large pot with just enough water to cover them. (Place a plate or other heavy object on top of the jars to keep them from floating.) Barely simmer for 15 minutes. Remove and cool at room temperature. By the next day, the centers of the metal lids should be suctioned downward and will not "pop" when you press them. Store the jars in your pantry until ready to use.

IF USING IMMEDIATELY:
Pour the jam into clean jars or containers and place in the refrigerator for up to a week.

YIELD ~ 5½ CUPS

> *We want to make sure our land stays strong and healthy for future generations.*
>
> —VICTOR RAMIREZ

California Strawberries 49

We are always trying to grow a better berry.

We pay attention to everything from the weather to the soil and how they are picked.

It is great that we grow something that makes people so happy.

—Victor Ramirez

Town Hall's philosophy is about using only the best ingredients mixed with lots of creativity. We have fun, and we want our customers to have fun.
  —Chefs Mitchell & Steven Rosenthal

Chefs Mitchell and Steven Rosenthal
California Strawberry & Currant Scones

INGREDIENTS
4 cups all-purpose flour
1 tablespoon baking powder
1 teaspoon baking soda
¾ cup sugar
½ teaspoon salt
2½ sticks butter (10 ounces),
   small cubes, cold
2 large eggs, *farm-fresh*
¾ cup buttermilk, *cold*
1½ teaspoons vanilla extract
1½ teaspoons orange extract
1 tablespoon strawberry preserves
   (See accompanying recipe.)
½ cup dried currants
2 cups whipped cream
2 cups fresh strawberries, *sliced*

PREPARATION
Preheat the oven to 400° F.

Mix together all of the dry ingredients. Cut the butter into the dry ingredients, and mix. In another bowl, combine the eggs, buttermilk, extracts, strawberry preserves, and currants.

Pour the wet ingredients over the dry, and stir together with a wooden spoon until combined. The mixture will be slightly bumpy.

With your hands, form the dough into 12 rounds and place on a baking sheet lined with parchment paper. Bake the scones for 20 minutes or until golden brown. Use a toothpick to ensure that the dough is cooked throughout.

Remove the scones from the oven and place on a cooling rack.

ON THE PLATE
Cut the scones in half lengthwise, and place a large dollop of whipped cream inside each. Top each scone with a generous helping of strawberries.

YIELD ~ 12 SCONES

SOURCING NOTES
California strawberries can be found year-round. As the warm coastal weather moves up the coastline, the berries come into season in various parts of the state. Look for California strawberries in your grocery store, where they will be designated by their place of origin: California.

KID-FRIENDLY COOKING
Many chefs will tell you that the best way to get kids interested in cooking is to get their hands into the process. Let the kids measure each ingredient. Instead of having them use a spoon, let their clean hands mix the ingredients, and have them whip the cream with a whisk. Kids are more inclined to eat something when they have a part in the process of preparing it. When they know the hard work that has gone into making a dish, they cherish it and respect it even more.

*I love cooking with strawberries—
everything from sweet to savory.*

—Chef Mitchell Rosenthal

Chef's Mitchell and Steven Rosenthal
Homemade Country Biscuits with Strawberries & Prosciutto

INGREDIENTS

1¼ cups all-purpose flour
1¼ cups cake flour
2 tablespoons baking flour
2¼ teaspoons salt
3 tablespoons sugar
2 sticks butter (½ pound), *cubed*
2 large farm eggs
1 cup buttermilk
1 stick butter, *softened*
Generous heap of thin-cut prosciutto, *or country ham*
1 cup strawberry preserves (See accompanying recipe.)

KID-FRIENDLY COOKING
Measuring provides a great opportunity for kids to brush up on their math. Use the many measurements in this recipe to help them understand fractions and build their math skills. This educational exercise also helps out the busy cook!

PREPARATION
Sift together all the dry ingredients. Combine them with the cubed ½ pound of butter, using a paddle mixer. Mix until combined. (The mixture will be coarse.)

One at a time, add the eggs to the dry ingredients. Stir in the buttermilk. Mix until just combined. (The dough will be moist and sticky.)

Fold the dough into one large mass and let it rest for at least 20 minutes.

Preheat the oven to 425° F.

Roll out the dough to a thickness of ½ inch. Cut out the biscuits in 2-inch rounds, using a cookie cutter or the open end of a drinking glass.

Place the biscuits on a baking sheet lined with parchment paper and let them rest for 10 minutes.

Bake the biscuits until golden brown, about 18 minutes. Remove them from the oven and let cool on a baking rack.

ON THE PLATE
Slice the biscuits in half lengthwise.

On a plate or platter, arrange the softened butter, several slices of thin-cut prosciutto (or country ham), strawberry preserves, and biscuits.

Let everyone serve themselves as follows: First, spread butter on the biscuit, then place prosciutto atop the butter, and finally, top with a generous portion of strawberry preserves. Close the biscuit and eat it like a sandwich.

YIELD ~ 25 SMALL BISCUITS

*In the kitchen I would just let the kids go wild—
You don't want them to be afraid of food, so just dive in!
Let them get involved in all of it; the cooking, the tasting, the eating.*
—Chef Steven Rosenthal

STRAWBERRY LEATHER ~
THAT'S FOR EATING, NOT WEARING!
Like all fruits, strawberries can be dried so that you can eat them anytime, even when they are not in season. One easy way to dry them is to make fruit leather. Older kids can do this recipe with minimal supervision.

WHAT YOU NEED
- Cookie Sheet
- Plastic wrap
- 1½ cups ripe strawberries
- Blender

WHAT YOU DO
- Line a cookie sheet with plastic wrap and set aside.
- Purée the strawberries in a blender.
- Pour the puree onto the cookie sheet and smooth the surface evenly.
- Place the cookie sheet into an oven set at its lowest temperature. Leave for 4 to 6 hours until the fruit has dried. (It will be slightly sticky to the touch and will peel easily from the plastic wrap.)
- While it's still warm, roll the dried fruit into a log and slice. Cover in plastic wrap and store at room temperature for up to 2 weeks.

These make a great snack at school, at work, or whenever you are on the run.

VITAL ELEMENTS ~ GET THEM HERE!
Vitamin C is an antioxidant. Antioxidants are thought to contribute to healthy skin and may help protect against heart disease and some forms of cancer.

When we think about sources of vitamin C, most of us think of oranges and other citrus fruits. But other fruits, strawberries among them, are also high in vitamin C, especially on a per-calorie basis. Strawberries are also packed with other antioxidants, including vitamins A and E, beta-carotene, selenium, and lycopene.

- Compare the vitamin C content of strawberries with the vitamin C in other fruits:

FRUIT	PORTION	CALORIES	MG. OF VITAMIN C
strawberries*	1 cup	45	85
apple	1 cup	62	4
grapes	10	36	5
tomato	1 cup	24	22
avocado	1 cup	370	18
navel orange	1 med.	65	47
blueberries	1 cup	82	19
raspberries	1 cup	61	31
kiwi fruit	1 med.	46	75

*One cup of strawberries satisfies the daily requirement of vitamin C.

FACTOID ~
HOW DO YOUR STRAWBERRIES GROW?
- **How many varieties of strawberries are there?**
  - 1—10
  - 31—51
  - 61—81
  - Hundreds

Answer: Hundreds. There are hundreds of known varieties of strawberries, with more varieties being discovered and created all the time.

- **What is the strawberry capital of the United States?**
  - Florida
  - California
  - Vermont
  - Louisiana

Answer: California, which grows more than 80 percent of all the strawberries grown in the United States.

WHAT IS A FRUIT? ~ ONE SEEDY PROPOSITION
Most people would identify a strawberry as a fruit. But not all fruits are commonly thought of as fruits—tomatoes, string beans, and cucumbers, for example. What makes a fruit a fruit? Botanically, a fruit is the seed-bearing part of a plant. Strawberries carry their seeds on the outside, while most fruits carry their seeds on the inside.

Fruit or Veggie?
- Make a list of as many fruits and vegetables as you can, and put each in its correct category—"fruit," "vegetable," or "both." "Both" refers to fruits that are used as vegetables, such as tomatoes, and vegetables that are used as fruits, such as rhubarb.

DYEING FOR SOME STRAWBERRIES ~
TIE-DYE BERRIES

Strawberry juice is a good dye. If you drip strawberry juice on your clothes, you may find that it doesn't wash out completely. Put the staining power of strawberry juice to good use with this dyeing activity. You may be surprised by the color you get.

WHAT YOU NEED
FOR THE FIXATIVE (TO SET THE DYE IN THE FABRIC)
- ½ cup salt added to 8 cups cold water
- Large pot

FOR THE DYE
- Rubber gloves
- 1 pint ripe strawberries
- Measuring cup
- Water
- Cheesecloth
- Large spoon
- Tongs

FOR THE FABRIC
- Wool, cotton, or other natural fabric

WHAT YOU DO
- Prepare a fixative by mixing the water and salt in a pot large enough to hold the fabric to be dyed.
- Simmer the fabric in the fixative for 1 hour.
- Remove the fabric, using the tongs, and squeeze out the fixative. Rinse the fabric thoroughly in cold water.
- Wear rubber gloves to protect your hands from the fixative and dye.
- Remove the stems from the berries. Crush the strawberries using a fork or potato masher. Measure the berries and add twice as much water as there are berries. Simmer the mixture for an hour or until the strawberries have lost their color. Strain out the dyeing liquid through the cheesecloth.
- Simmer the rinsed fabric in the dye for 30 to 60 minutes until the desired color is reached, occasionally turning the fabric gently in the dye bath, using a large spoon. (Strawberries dye a fabric pink. The finished color is always lighter than the color in the dye bath.)
- Rinse the dyed fabric with cool water and hang to dry. Experiment with other berries to see what colors they produce.

DESIGNER FRUIT ~
INVENT YOUR OWN SWEET STUFF
- Talk about the fruits you like, and what you like about them.
- If you could combine all the characteristics you like into one fruit, what would the new fruit look like and taste like? What would you name it, and how would you advertise it?

BERRY SWEET STUFF ~
STRAWBERRY FACTS
- If you were to line up all of the strawberries produced in California in one year, side by side, they would wrap around the world 15 times!
- A serving of eight medium strawberries has 93 percent of your recommended daily allowance of vitamin C.
- Today, strawberries represent a $1.1 billion industry in California.
- There is an average of 200 seeds in every strawberry.

ACTIVITIES

Artisan Chèvre

featuring

CHEF BRUCE SHERMAN
NORTH POND RESTAURANT   CHICAGO, ILLINOIS

ANNE TOPHAM
FANTÔME FARM   RIDGEWAY, WISCONSIN

RINK DAVEE
SHOOTING STAR FARM   MINERAL POINT, WISCONSIN

Acclaimed chef
Bruce Sherman was headed for a career in banking and finance before he decided to enter the restaurant world.

Cheese maker Anne Topham was studying for her doctorate when she visited her grandparents' farm and decided never to return to academic life.

In this culinary sojourn, Chef Sherman, and his two young daughters join Anne in the rolling hills of southern Wisconsin to milk goats and make farmstead cheese.

The children get an early lesson in kid psychology as Anne explains, *"The goats are a whole lot smarter than cows—they are very independent creatures."*

The chef and his kids discover how Anne's relationship with the animals and the land carries through in the taste of her award-winning cheeses; they're extremely fresh, always beautiful and full-flavored but never "goaty." From milking the herd to carefully hand-crafting the cheese, Chef Sherman and daughters learn the art, and rewards, of patience.

Then the group heads down the road to the farm of Rink DaVee, one of Wisconsin's most-prized farmers, to gather some carefully grown herbs and greens to accompany their freshly made Fantôme Farm goat cheese.

Chef Bruce Sherman
Apple & Chèvre Double-Stuffed Delicata Squash Boats

INGREDIENTS
2 medium delicata squash
2 tablespoons canola oil
Salt and white pepper, *to taste*
½ cup apple cider, *fresh-pressed, preferably unfiltered*
½ cup apple cider vinegar
¼ cup maple syrup
1 large seasonal apple, *peeled, cored, ¼" dice*
½ cup fresh Parmesan cheese, *grated*
½ cup fresh breadcrumbs
4 ounces fresh goat cheese
¼ cup pecans, *toasted and chopped*
1 tablespoon unsalted butter, *chilled*

SOURCING NOTES
The delicata squash is a lush, oblong squash with cream-colored skin and forest-green stripes. Its creamy flavor and small size make it ideal for this dish. But don't feel that you have to use the delicata variety. Look for other fun varieties that may be in season in your area. Often, new and unusual varieties can be spotted at your local market. But be sure to ask your purveyor if the flesh is "soft," as you won't want to use a squash with "stringy" consistency.

PREPARATION
Preheat the oven to 350°F. Slice the squash in half, end to end. Rub all surfaces of the squash with the canola oil. Season with salt and pepper. Place the squash on a cookie sheet, cut side up, and roast for 30 to 40 minutes, until the flesh yields easily to the touch.

While the squash bakes, place the cider and cider vinegar in a small, non-reactive saucepan on medium heat. Bring to a boil, reduce and simmer until 3 tablespoons of syrup remain. Turn off the heat. Reserve, keeping the mixture warm.

In a separate saucepan, cook the maple syrup over high heat for 2 minutes, or until it's reduced by half. Add the diced apple to the syrup and toss to coat it entirely, cooking 1 minute more. Remove and reserve.

Mix the grated cheese and breadcrumbs together in a small bowl. Set aside.

Remove the squash from the oven and carefully scoop out and discard the seeds from the central cavity. Next, scoop out the flesh, trying to avoid penetrating the skin. Reserve the squash hulls.

Place the squash flesh in a mixing bowl and mix in the reserved maple-apple pieces, the goat cheese, toasted pecans, and ¼ cup of the mixed cheese and breadcrumbs. Season to taste.

"Stuff" the mixture back into the squash hulls and dust the squash liberally with the remainder of the breadcrumb mix. Place back in the oven. Bake the squash boats an additional 15 minutes, until the tops are lightly browned. When ready to serve, gently heat the cider-vinegar reduction and whisk in the butter.

ON THE PLATE
If serving the squash boats as an appetizer, cut them in half. Place the squash in the center of the plate. Drizzle the apple vinegar sauce alongside. Serve warm.

YIELD ~ 4 APPETIZER PORTIONS OR 2 MAIN COURSES

It's about communities, connections, sources, and people.

It's about tasting the cheese and seeing a face.

It's about honoring the commitment of the people who lovingly grow and nurture our food.

　　　-Chef Bruce Sherman

Artisan Chèvre **61**

There are better ways of sourcing food, cooking food, eating food: It doesn't have to be the American notion of cheap and fast.

Locally produced food may be a little more expensive, it may be harder to procure, but it tastes better and is better for you. It's a better choice to make. ...

This is an ideal that rubs off on the kids, for sure.

—Chef Bruce Sherman

Artisan Chèvre 63

Chef Bruce Sherman
Apple-Leek Soup with Herbed Goat Cheese Gnocchi and a Nest of Fresh Spinach

INGREDIENTS

FOR THE SOUP

3 medium-large leeks
1 tablespoon canola oil
1 whole shallot, *peeled, thinly sliced*
1 rib celery, *¼" dice*
2 medium local apples, *peeled, cored, ½" dice*
1/3 cup white wine
3 cups chicken or vegetable stock or water
4 tablespoons unsalted butter
Salt and white pepper, *to taste*

for the gnocchi
1 cup goat cheese, *packed firmly*
¼ lemon, *zest only*
2 teaspoons extra virgin olive oil
½ cup Parmesan cheese, *grated*
1 tablespoon fresh Italian parsley, *chopped*
2 teaspoons chives, *finely chopped*
1 teaspoon mint, *finely chopped*
½ teaspoon tarragon, *leaves finely chopped*
¼ cup pastry flour, *measured, and sifted*
1 farm egg
Salt and white pepper, *to taste*

FOR THE PRESENTATION
Spinach, *thinly shredded.*
Croutons
¼ cup cooked bacon, *diced*

PREPARATION

FOR THE SOUP:

Halve the white leek bottoms and wash *very* well in a cold-water bath. Thinly slice them and reserve. Cut the leek greens into 1-to-1½" pieces and wash them. Reserve.

In a medium sauce pot, heat the canola or vegetable oil over medium heat. Add in the leek whites, shallot, and celery. Add salt and pepper, and stir for 3 minutes until the vegetables soften. Add in the apples and cook for an additional 3 minutes. Add in the wine and cook for 2 more minutes. Add in the stock or water, bring to a boil, and simmer gently for 5 minutes. Taste the broth and season heavily with additional salt, if necessary.

Place the mixture in a blender (with the hole open in the top cover to allow steam to escape) and *carefully* blend until the mixture is entirely smooth. Pass through a fine-mesh strainer and discard the solids. Reserve.

Put the cut leek tops in a large pot of heavily salted, boiling water. Boil for 3 minutes, then strain and remove to an ice-water bath. Strain and place the cold pieces of leek in the blender. Blend on high for 3 minutes or until an emulsion is made and the mixture is a viscous green purée. Pass through a fine-mesh strainer and discard the solids. Reserve.

FOR THE GNOCCHI:
Place the goat cheese, lemon zest, olive oil, chopped herbs, and salt and pepper, to taste, in a bowl, and mix until smooth. Mix in the egg and Parmesan. Add the flour, and mix until it's just incorporated. Cover with plastic wrap, and allow it to rest in the refrigerator.

ON THE PLATE

Heat the soup base in a pot. When it's simmering, add in the butter, and season to taste. Using a small melon scoop, drop the gnocchi, one at a time, into water that's just barely simmering, and cookuntil they begin to float, about 1 minute. Remove the gnocchi from the water and place evenly among 4 serving bowls. Season to taste. Place a clump of shredded spinach in the middle of each bowl and sprinkle with croutons (forming a "nest" of spinach). "Finish" the soup by adding the green leek-top purée at the last minute and adjusting the seasoning. Pour into the soup bowls. Sprinkle bacon bits atop the soup. Serve immediately.

YIELD ~ 4 SERVINGS

*Ohhh, this is so good.
...I knew it would be delicious.*

–Kate Sherman

Artisan Chèvre

SMILE & SAY CHEESE! ~
MAKE YOUR OWN CHEESE AT HOME

Making fresh cheese at home is simple. All you need is milk, heat, and something acidic, such as lemon juice or vinegar.

Whole milk makes the best-tasting cheese, but you can also use lower-fat milk. (You can't, however, use heavy cream, because it has no proteins from which to form curds.)

Adding lemon juice or vinegar to warm milk causes the milk protein to clump into curds and separate from the liquid, called "whey." (Now you understand what Little Miss Muffet was eating.) The drained curds are the cheese. Ricotta cheese, farmer's cheese, and Indian paneer are all made this way.

WHAT YOU NEED
- Large saucepan
- 1 quart milk
- 1 tablespoon lemon juice
- pinch of salt (optional)
- Cheesecloth
- Sieve or strainer

WHAT YOU DO
- Rinse out the saucepan with water. Do not dry it. (The water keeps the milk from burning in the pan.)
- Bring the milk to a boil in the saucepan. Be careful to not let the milk boil over.
- Remove the pan from the heat, add the lemon juice, and add the salt if desired.
- Stir until the curds separate from the whey.
- Let sit for 15 to 30 minutes to allow the curds to fully develop.
- Strain the mixture through a cheesecloth-lined sieve or strainer.
- When the curds are cool enough to handle, gather the edges of the cheesecloth together and squeeze out the remaining moisture. Your cheese is now ready to serve.

SERVING IDEAS
Use the cheese as a spread topped with herbs or jam. Mix with sour cream or yogurt and herbs to use as a dip with crackers.

ALL IN THE FAMILY ~ MEET THE ALLIUMS

The onion family (*Alliaceae* or *Allium*) has many members that have bulbs used in cooking, each with a different flavor. Among them are: garlic, leeks, scallions, shallots, and white, yellow, and red onions.

WHAT YOU DO
- Gather as many members of the onion family as possible.
- What do they all have in common?
- Compare the size, color, smell, and taste of each.
- Chop each type. Which members of the family make you cry?
- Sauté each in vegetable oil, and taste. How does cooking alter the taste?

Chives are also members of the onion family. How does their use differ from that of all of their cousins? Are there any other *Allium* relatives that you can think of?

Cheese should be served slightly warm or at room temperature ... so that you can experience the full taste and subtle nuances.

—Anne Topham

ENDLESS SUMMER ~ PRESERVING THE HARVEST

The enjoyment of fresh herbs can be extended by using them to flavor vinegars. Tarragon vinegar is especially good on salads.

WHAT YOU NEED
- 1 quart white vinegar
- ½ cup sugar
- 1 large bunch tarragon
- 20 black peppercorns, left whole

WHAT YOU DO
- Bring the vinegar and the sugar to a boil, and simmer 5 minutes.
- Wash and dry the tarragon (the leaves can be left on the stems), and put the tarragon and peppercorns in a clean, dry glass quart jar.
- Pour the boiled vinegar over the tarragon in the jar. Cover. Store in the refrigerator.

DRY YOUR CRYIN' EYES ~ WEEP NO MORE

Cutting raw onions can make your eyes tear. Why? Because onions contain a chemical irritant that is released when the onion is cut.

When you slice through an onion, you break open cells that have enzymes inside of them. The enzymes, called amino acid sulfoxides, rearrange themselves to form a mild sulfuric acid, a volatile gas that irritates the eyes. The nerve endings in your eyes are very sensitive so they pick up on this irritation. The brain reacts by telling your tear ducts to produce more water, to dilute the irritating acid so the eyes are protected. But don't rub your eyes—it will only make the reaction worse!

There are several suggested ways to avoid crying over cut onions, however. Try them. Which ones work for you?

- Cut the onion under running water.
- Chew on bread, chewing gum, or taffy while cutting the onion.
- Don't cut through the root end, which contains most of the chemical.
- Refrigerate the onion for at least 30 minutes before you cut it.
- Cut a cone out of the root end of the onion, about one-third the diameter of the onion and one-third as deep.
- Chop the onion in a food processor, but stand back when you open the processor.
- Use a sharp (not blunt) knife for chopping.
- Wear a pair of ski goggles to protect your eyes. They may look funny, but many swear that they work!

THE NOSE KNOWS ~ IS TASTE RELATED TO SMELL?

Use your sense of smell to try to recognize some common foods.

WHAT YOU DO

- Gather an assortment of foods with distinctive odors, such as banana, cinnamon, chocolate, lemon, orange, onion, and peanut butter. Dust a cotton ball with the cinnamon, and peel the fruits and onion. Place a small amount of each food in individual dishes, keeping the foods out of sight of the guesser. Give each person a turn at trying to recognize the foods just by smell. As necessary, you can let them taste, too.
- Which foods are easiest to recognize by smell? Which have the most-distinct smells?

FACTOID ~
OUR FOUR-FOOTED FRIENDS GET A LITTLE "CHEESEY"

Cheese can be made from any kind of milk, but the cheeses you are most likely to see for sale come from cows, sheep, goats, and buffalo.

- How many of these cheeses can you find?
- How do their tastes compare?
- Which are your favorites?
- Think about what you would pair with each type of cheese.

FEELING FRUITY ~ BLOCK PRINTS FROM FRUITS & VEGETABLES

You don't need a paintbrush to create a work of art. Fruits and vegetables such as apples and potatoes make excellent artists' tools. You can easily make block prints using the ingredients in your kitchen.

WHAT YOU DO

- Lay out several whole potatoes, squash, and/or apples. Slice each open. (Try experimenting with cutting lengthwise, around, or in various shapes.) Look at the inside of each. What unique patterns do they have? What characteristics does each have?
- Pour tempera or fabric paint onto small paper plates or into recycled bowls. Dip the various foods in the paint, and place them on fabric or paper. Each item will give you a unique print that resembles the veins, seeds, and flesh inside. If desired, carefully cut the potato into various forms and shapes.

Try making block prints on cloth napkins for a unique party addition, or on canvas bags that you can reuse every time you go shopping. Create cards for your next party, by using recycled paper. These are not only fun, but good for the environment as well.

Saving Seeds & Heirloom Veggies

featuring

CHEF JOSEPH WREDE
JOSEPH'S TABLE   TAOS, NEW MEXICO

KELLE CARTER
RANCHO LA PAZ FARM   SAN JUAN PUEBLO, NEW MEXICO

Considered one of the Southwest's modern culinary pioneers, Chef Joseph Wrede creates classic dishes with chile pepper flair at Taos' esteemed Joseph's Table restaurant.

The chef and his two children pull on their boots for a day of discovery at Rancho la Paz, a tiny but glorious farm nestled along the Rio Grande in the southern Rocky Mountains, tended by the hands of grower Kelle Carter.

Chef and children discover that the bounty is ripe for the picking at this experimental organic farm as they attempt to sample ninety-six kinds of tomatoes, thirty-two types of basil, and forty-seven varieties of sweet and spicy peppers.

When they venture into a magical tunnel of gourds, the children are transported into the pages of a fairy tale. Then Chef Wrede and farmer Kelle help the kids plant next season's harvest, offering a lesson in how to nurture and preserve seeds for the future.

Chef Joseph Wrede
Six-Tomato Summer Gazpacho

INGREDIENTS
- 6 medium organic vine-ripened tomatoes, *of various varieties*
- 2 red bell peppers
- 5 garlic cloves, *roughly chopped*
- 2 red onions, *peeled and roughly chopped*
- 3 cucumbers, *peeled and seeded*
- 2 ears corn, *roasted, with kernels sliced off ears*
- 4 tablespoons extra virgin olive oil
- 2 tablespoons red wine vinegar
- Salt and pepper, *to taste*

PREPARATION
Seed, peel, and roughly chop the tomatoes. NOTE: If you are using a cherry variety, use a small handful that is about equal to the meat of one medium tomato. You should have about 4 cups of tomatoes after they are peeled and seeded.

Roast the red bell peppers by placing them over a flame or under the broiler. If using a broiler, let the skins blister and blacken, turning the peppers so that they are charred on all sides. Once the peppers are blackened, place in a metal bowl and cover with plastic wrap. Let sit 5 minutes. Peel and seed the peppers.

Place all of the ingredients in a blender. Pulse until smooth consistency is achieved. NOTE: Because you are using a variety of tomatoes, the color will vary dramatically each time you make the gazpacho. Hold a few bright red tomatoes in reserve and add them to the blender to brighten up the color, if needed.

Adjust to taste with salt and pepper.

ON THE PLATE
Fill four bowls with gazpacho. Garnish with crème fraîche and additional slices of tomato, if desired.

YIELD ~ 4 SERVINGS

SOURCING NOTES
Tomatoes, tomatoes, tomatoes! This gazpacho offers a great opportunity to experiment with the many fun varieties that are now available. To maximize the flavor of this gazpacho, use locally grown tomatoes that are super sweet and just picked.

Oftentimes, farmers at the market will hold boxes of "second tomatoes" aside. These are usually a bit bumped or bruised, but because you are blending the tomatoes, the appearance doesn't matter. So ask your local farmer for a variety box of "seconds." It will save you money and help a farmer put his crops to good use.

KID-FRIENDLY COOKING
Let the kids create their own works of art by decorating the gazpacho with crème fraîche hair, sliced tomatoes for eyes, and a drizzle of olive oil for a smile.

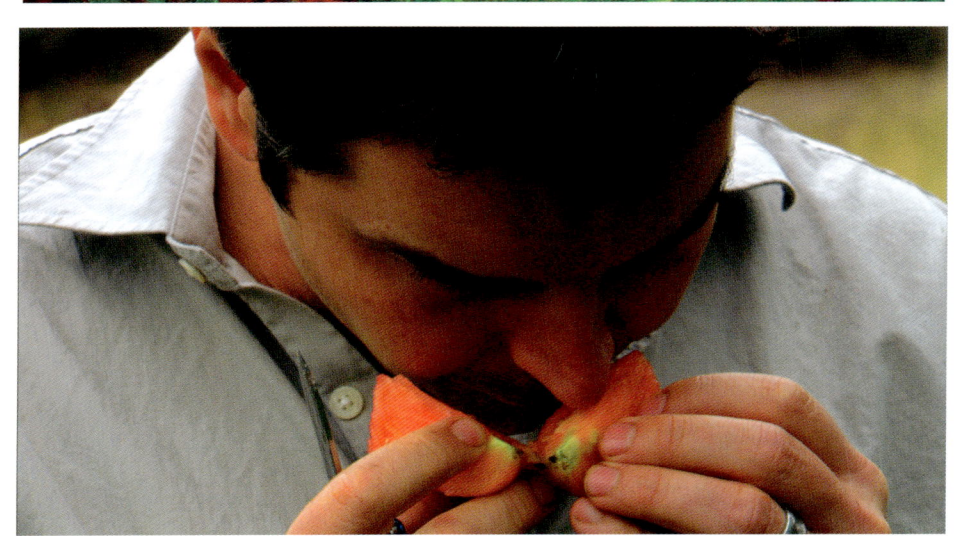

We need to remember that this country was built on agriculture.

Now we need to turn our attention away from chefs and back toward the farm. ...
—Chef Joseph Wrede

Saving Seeds & Heirloom Veggies 71

What turns me on in the kitchen is improvisation and building flavor— allowing your imagination to run wild.

It's funny, when you cook with your kids, how quickly that process takes off.

—Chef Joseph Wrede

Chef Joseph Wrede
Herbaceous Fried Shrimp

PREPARATION

In a sauté pan, heat the oil until hot. Add the rosemary, thyme, parsley, sage, and garlic, and heat for 2 minutes.

Turn the herbs over and add the shrimp, cooking it for 2 minutes per side.

Toast the bread. Pour the oil from the herb-shrimp pan evenly over the bread.

ON THE PLATE

Cut the bread in half on the diagonal and put on a plate. Pile the shrimp and fried herbs on top. Serve with a ramekin of balsamic vinegar for dipping.

YIELD ~ 1 SERVING

INGREDIENTS

3 tablespoons olive oil
1 sprig fresh rosemary
1 sprig fresh thyme
1 sprig fresh flat-leaf parsley
1 leaf fresh sage
1 clove garlic, *crushed with back of knife blade*
6 jumbo shrimp
1 piece toasted bread, *highest-quality bread available*
2 tablespoons aged balsamic vinegar

KID-FRIENDLY COOKING

Creating a kitchen that is kid-friendly will encourage the kids to get involved. A sturdy stool that brings small hands up to the height of the counter will work for older children. But, for younger ones, don't be afraid to sit them on the counter (be sure to keep a close eye on them), take the ingredients to a kitchen table that is more manageable to reach, or even lay out a picnic blanket on a clean kitchen floor and bring the utensils and tools to their level. (One extra advantage of cooking "picnic" style is that you can simply bundle up the dirty blanket and put it straight into the wash!) Let everyone help in the shopping, the cooking, the cleanup, and of course the eating. You will quickly learn that making a homemade meal can be a great source of family fun and quality time spent together.

SOME SEEDY BUSINESS ~
SOWING & SAVING SEEDS

The next time you cut into a really luscious tomato, whether from a farm or your home garden, try saving its seeds for planting next year. You can save the seeds of many plants. But be sure to store the seeds in a cool, dry spot until you can plant them.

Basil seeds are especially easy to collect. Once the flower head on the basil plant has turned brown, snip it off and suspend it upside down with a binder clip in a paper envelope. The seeds, which are very tiny, will fall off (or you will have to rub them off if they are stubborn). Plant the seeds as part of an indoor herb garden.

You can create your own unique garden by saving and sowing various seeds. During the summer, try allowing a few of the herb plants in your garden to "go to seed" by letting them flower, instead of picking the herbs. Save and dry the seeds. Now you are ready to start growing your own special herb garden. Here's how you do it:

- Gather the saved seeds from a variety of herbs, keeping them separate.
- Put 2 inches of potting soil in a shallow container, such as a terra cotta pot, that is 10 to 12 inches in diameter. Or reuse a plastic egg carton or "clamshell" (the kind of container that salad greens and fruits such as strawberries are often sold in).
- Lightly score the surface of the soil with a pencil tip, dividing it into as many sections as you have seed varieties. Sprinkle one kind of seed in each section. Sprinkle a thin layer of soil on top of the seeds. Water lightly. Loosely cover with a piece of plastic wrap to keep the soil moist but not soggy.
- Keep the planter out of direct sunlight until the seeds have sprouted. Water the seedlings when the soil surface feels dry. Remove the plastic wrap once the seedlings have sprouted.
- When the seedlings have four or more leaves, thin them to about 2 inches apart by cutting out any unhealthy seedlings. Move to a sunny window.
- In summer, transplant the herbs to a large outdoor pot or space for an herb garden of your own.

THE WELL-READ PLANT ~
HOMEMADE POTS TO HELP YOUR GARDEN GROW

To start seeds indoors, you don't need pots from the garden center. You can use newspaper to make biodegradable pots that can be put directly into the ground once the seedlings are ready to be planted.

WHAT YOU NEED
- Newspaper
- Unopened vegetable can,
- Unopened can or jar

WHAT YOU DO
- Fold one page of the newspaper in half lengthwise.
- Place the top of the larger can along the folded edge of the newspaper.
- Roll the newspaper loosely around the can.
- Fold in the overhanging end of the newspaper.
- Slide the can out about ¾ inch.
- Press the bottom of the wrapped can against the top of the smaller can and twist several times to compress the newspaper.
- Remove the larger can.
- Trim the top of the pot to the desired height.
- Fill the pot with soil when you're ready to plant your seeds.

MORE IDEAS FOR MAKING SEED POTS

Try recycling old egg cartons by making seed pots out of the bottoms of the cartons. If you're using plastic egg cartons, poke a small hole in the bottom of each cup so excess water can drain out; use the top of the carton as a saucer under the bottom. You can also make seed pots from the plastic "clamshells" used to package fruits and vegetables.

Taste is one of the most important things we strive for. If something tastes good, it will continue to be propogated, people will, hopefully, continue to want to grow it, even if it's not the perfect shape or color.

–Kelle Carter

HIGH AND DRY ~
MAKE SUN-DRIED TOMATOES AT HOME

Drying food is one of the oldest ways of preserving it, and sun-dried tomatoes are popular. But food simply left out to dry runs a race with mold. To dry tomatoes faster than mold can catch up with them, you can make a simple food dryer.

WHAT YOU NEED
- Sturdy cardboard carton with a removable lid
- Scissors or knife
- Clean nylon screen or plastic mesh
- Tape
- Black construction paper or poster paint
- Plastic food wrap
- Tomatoes

WHAT YOU DO
TO MAKE THE DRYER

The dryer consists of two parts: a mesh-covered base to hold the tomatoes and a top that concentrates heat from the sun.
- The lid of the box becomes the base for holding the food to be dried. To make "feet" for the base, cut rectangular pieces out of the sides of the lid. Begin cutting 2 inches from the corners and cut halfway up the side. (Repeat on all four sides.)
- Make the drying surface: Cut the screen or mesh to the same dimensions as the lid, and put aside. Cut out the center of the lid, leaving a 2 inch border all around. Tape the screen over the hole in the lid.
- The bottom of the box becomes the "oven." Turn the box over so that the open end is down. Cut across one of the long edges of the box horizontally. Cut along the shorter sides at a 45-degree angle to the first cut until you reach the other long side. Cut across the long side to remove the piece.
- Paint the inside of the "oven" with black paint or cover it with black construction paper.
- Cover the angled opening with plastic wrap, and secure with tape.

TO PREPARE THE TOMATOES
- Dip whole, ripe tomatoes in boiling water for about 30 seconds to loosen the skin.
- Peel the tomatoes, cut into ½-inch-thick slices, and remove the seeds.
- Place the slices of tomato on the screen or mesh.
- Top with the plastic-covered box.
- Place the dryer outside, facing in the direction that gets the most sunlight. Leave the tomatoes in the dryer for one to two days.
- Test your tomato slices for dryness—they should be pliable but should not have any moisture—before you store them in the refrigerator.

HOT TOMATO! ~
TOMATO BASKETS & CHILE PEPPER FLOWERS

WHAT YOU NEED
- Firm, fresh, large tomato
- Paring knife
- Assorted colors and sizes of chile peppers, with stems attached
- Scissors
- Bowl with cold water
- Fresh basil and other leafy herbs

WHAT YOU DO
FOR THE TOMATO BASKET
- If the tomato does not sit straight on its stem end, cut off a thin slice.
- To create the basket "handle," work with the stem end down. Place your knife ¼ inch from the center of the tomato. Cut straight down to the middle of the tomato. Make a horizontal cut through the middle of the tomato to meet the vertical cut. Remove the wedge. Repeat on the other side of the tomato.
- Cut a sawtooth pattern into the "rim" of the basket from one side of the "handle" to the other.
- Scoop out the seeds and pulp.

FOR THE CHILE PEPPER FLOWERS
- Cut the tip off the chile pepper.
- With a pair of scissors, make at least four evenly spaced lengthwise cuts in the pepper.
- Remove the seeds and pulp. (Wear gloves if possible, and don't touch your eyes with your fingers after working with the peppers.)
- Soak the peppers in cold water so that the "petals" will open.
- Drain the "flowers" and fill the tomato basket with them. Add the fresh leafy herbs.

ACTIVITIES

chefsafield.com

PIE IN THE SKY ~
CREATE A RAINBOW ON YOUR PLATE
Having foods in a variety of colors on your plate looks good and is good for you. The colors (red, orange, green, yellow, and purple) reflect the vitamins and minerals in the food. Carrots and sweet potatoes, for example, are rich in vitamin A; blue and purple fruits are high in antioxidants.

Here are a few examples of how the color on the plate may be helping your health:

COLOR	EXAMPLE	NUTRIENT	POSSIBLE BENEFIT
red	tomato	lycopene	Reduce risks of some cancers.
red	raspberry	anthocyanins	Antioxidants protect cells from damage.
orange/yellow	carrot	beta-carotene	Maintain healthy eyes.
blue/purple	grape	anthocyanins	Antioxidants protect cells from damage.
green	leafy greens	folate	B vitamin keeps heart healthy.

* What color foods do you eat the most of? Which color is your favorite? Which do you need to eat more of?
* Try to increase the colors of your foods: Assign each day of the week a color. Try eating vegetables and fruits from that color group each day. At the end of the week, see if you have eaten all of the colors of the rainbow.
* When shopping at the grocery store or market, take a colored picture of the rainbow with you. See if you can find fruits and vegetables to correspond to each color.
* Make your plate a rainbow: Using color pencils or pens, decorate 7 paper plates, each with various colors of the rainbow. (Be sure to use them all!) Label each plate with a day of the week. Each night at dinner, create a meal that includes the various colors that you have painted on your plate. By the end of the week, you will have eaten a rainbow of colors and flavors.

THERE'S NO "THYME" TO WAIT! ~
QUICK-DRIED HERBS
Small quantities of herbs can be dried in the microwave so that you can use them year-round. It's simple to do.

WHAT YOU NEED
- Fresh herbs
- Paper towels
- Small bowl with water
- Microwave oven

WHAT YOU DO
* Herbs have their best flavor before they produce flowers. And for drying, it is best to pick herbs early in the day.
* Arrange three to five sprigs of herbs between 2 paper towels.
* Place the herbs and a small bowl of water in the microwave.
* Microwave on HIGH for 2 to 3 minutes.
* Check for dryness. The leaves should crumble easily. If additional time is needed, microwave in 30-second intervals.
* Store in an airtight container.

Use your dried herbs in place of fresh. But remember that dried herbs are more concentrated in flavor and require you to use less in a recipe.

> *I think it's important that food not only looks good, but tastes good.*
> –CHEF JOSEPH WREDE

BUTTERFLY FLUTTER ~
CREATE A BUTTERFLY GARDEN

Butterflies are attracted to particular plants for their smell, taste, and color. Flowers with bright colors such as red, yellow, and purple are particularly attractive to butterflies. Try planting some butterfly-friendly plants in your garden:

aster	Joe-Pye weed
bee balm	marigold
milkweed	clover
nasturtium	parsley
cosmos	verbena
daisies	violets
zinnia	carrots

* See if you can watch the whole butterfly life cycle in your garden. Look for tiny eggs on the undersides of leaves on "host" plants such as daisies, milkweed, parsley, and clover. Later, you should see caterpillars on the same plants. You might even see a chrysalis. Look for these hanging from a twig or stem, but be careful not to disturb them, so metamorphosis can take place.

DRINK UP ~ DRINKING PLANTS

The roots of a plant take up water from the soil. You can see this with a regular carrot, which is the root of a carrot plant.

WHAT YOU NEED
- Blue food coloring
- Cup of water
- Carrot

WHAT YOU DO
* Mix a few drops of the food coloring into the cup of water.
* Place the carrot in the water.
* After waiting a few hours, pull the carrot out and cut off a small section near the tip.
* Look at both the carrot and the piece you cut off. You should see blue dots on the inside sections of these 2 pieces. The blue dots indicate where the water is being carried through the root.

The roots bring water and nutrients up into the plant through hollow tubes as shown by the blue food coloring. Water and nutrients are essential for a plant to grow.

* Cut off another piece of carrot, looking for the same blue dots again. Keep cutting sections off the carrot. How far did the water travel up the carrot?

* Think about what else plants may carry through their roots. How does this relate to pesticide and chemical use on plants?

* Try the experiment with other vegetables, such as a celery stock, to see what the results are.

ACTIVITIES

FARMERS MARKET SCAVENGER HUNT

HOW DOES YOUR GARDEN GROW? ~
FUN AT THE FARMERS MARKET

At a farmers market, the offerings change each week. Taking a trip to the market is a fun way to see what's in season and to try new things. Try this scavenger hunt the next time you visit the farmers market.

- What is today's date?
- What season does that mean it is?
- What region of the country are you in?

- List five fruits and five vegetables that are available at the farmers market right now.

   Fruits:

   Vegetables:

- Name three fruits or vegetables that come in several different varieties, colors, or types at the farmers market.

- Find and name three of the varieties.

- Name three fruits or vegetables you usually see at the grocery store that you don't see here.

- Why do you think it isn't here?

- What is your favorite fruit or vegetable available at the market today?
  (Sample at least one new thing with each visit!)

- Name one fruit or vegetable in the market that you've never seen before.

- Draw a picture of it:

- Ask a farmer if you can taste a sample. Describe the taste.

- Does it remind you of any other fruits or vegetables?

- Do you see any other products besides fruits and vegetables?
  What are some examples?
  Where are they made or grown?

GET TO KNOW A GROWER ~
TALK TO A FARMER

Find a farmer at your local farmers market and ask him or her a few questions. (You may be surprised by how much farmers like to talk and share information!)

Suggested questions for the farmer:
- What is your name?
- What is the name of your farm?
- Where is your farm located? Where is that, from here?
- What kinds of things do you grow or raise on your farm?
- How long have you been a farmer?
- Why did you decide to be a farmer?
- How do you take care of your soil and land?
- What are some things you do to make things grow well on your farm?
- Is your farm organic? What does organic mean?
- What does sustainability mean?
- Do you like being a farmer?
- What do you like most about being a farmer?
- What is the hardest part about being a farmer?
- What is your favorite season?
- What is your favorite food to eat? To grow?
- What is the most delicious thing you are selling today?

Take the scavenger hunt on various trips to the market.

✳ Do you get different answers during different parts of the season? Which season is your favorite? Do you have a favorite market or a favorite farmer you like to visit at the market?

STOP BUGGIN' ME ~ BATTLE OF THE BUGS... 'GOOD VERSUS BAD'
A lot of people think all bugs are pests. But organic farmers know that some bugs can be powerful helpers on the farm. These bugs are called "beneficial Insects." On an organic farm, the farmer uses "*good*" bugs to fight off "*bad bugs*" and disease. Using bugs means that they don't have to use poisonous pesticides or chemicals. Here is a list of bugs that can commonly be found on a farm. Each bug has something to say. Circle the "good" bugs and cross out the "bad" bugs that eat crops:

- THRIP *I suck the juice from leaves, fruits, and vegetables. I like to lay my eggs in summer fruits like tomatoes and strawberries.*
- LADYBUG *I love to eat aphids, and my children do, too. Mmm good!*
- APHID *I am very thirsty. I suck juice from leaves, flowers, vegetables, and fruits to give me energy.*
- CABBAGE LOOPER LARVA *I will grow up to be an adult by eating lots of fresh, green vegetables like cabbage.*
- ASSASSIN BUG *Yum! I like to jump on aphids and eat them. They are delicious!*
- LACEWING LARVA *While I'm growing, I like to eat yummy bugs like aphids! I prefer bugs to leaves.*
- PARASITIC WASP *I lay my eggs inside aphids. When the eggs hatch, my children have aphids to eat! They are delicious and help my children grow big.*

※ Look for ladybugs and other "*good*" bugs in your yard. Visit your local garden store to find out about other natural ways to keep your garden growing, without chemicals, but instead, using natural defenses such as "*good*" bugs.

※ Catch bugs from your garden using a glass jar. Compare your bugs to a reference book so that you can see who is flying around your garden. Are there any common physical characteristics of "good" bugs? Which are most plentiful? Make a list of what kinds of bugs are in your garden— check back during different times of the season to see if you can find new species. (Be sure to let the bugs go free, however—you will want to let them do their job!)

ACTIVITIES

Shrimp Boat on the Bayou

featuring

CHEF JOHN BESH
RESTAURANT AUGUST NEW ORLEANS, LOUISIANA
BESH STEAKHOUSE NEW ORLEANS, LOUISIANA
LÜKE NEW ORLEANS, LOUISIANA
LA PROVENCE LACOMBE, LOUISIANA

CAPTAIN LANCE NACIO
THE ANNA MARIE COCODRIE, LOUISIANA

What happens when a former Marine, a ten-year-old boy, and a bayou shrimp-boat captain get together for a day out at sea?

The Marine, Chef John Besh, and his son Brendan get an unexpected lesson in marine biology, and the captain, Lance Nacio, is let in on a few culinary secrets for preparing his freshly caught Louisiana wild shrimp.

The journey begins in the pitch-black pre-dawn hours on a sleepy Louisiana bayou. The waters come alive, offering a bounty of sea life and surprises.

The hard work of pulling in nets is second nature to Chef Besh, who grew up hunting and fishing in the area and is now one of America's most respected chefs.

Brendan is wide-eyed and all smiles as he sorts through a cornucopia of gigantic, fresh shrimp he can't wait to sink his teeth into.

Then it's into the kitchen, where Brendan and his dad show the rest of the family just how the cookin' is done in this Southern household.

Chef John Besh
The Besh Louisiana Barbeque Shrimp

INGREDIENTS

FOR THE BARBEQUE BASE

3 cups shrimp shells
3 cups water
3 cups Worcestershire sauce
1 teaspoon plus 1 tablespoon black pepper, *divided*
1 teaspoon Creole seasoning
¼ teaspoon cloves
1 bay leaf
1 tablespoon lemon juice

FOR THE SHRIMP

2 pounds jumbo Louisiana wild-caught shrimp, *preferably with heads on*
1 tablespoon olive oil
2 teaspoons salt
1 tablespoon black pepper
1½ cups heavy cream
1½ cups melted butter
1 large loaf of bread

PREPARATION

FOR THE BARBEQUE BASE:

In a heavy-bottomed saucepan, lightly toast the shrimp shells for 5 minutes over very high heat. Add the water, Worcestershire sauce, 1 teaspoon black pepper, Creole seasoning, cloves, bay leaf, and lemon juice. Bring to a simmer and let the liquid reduce by half.

FOR THE SHRIMP:

In another large pot, sauté the shrimp for about 2 minutes in the olive oil, over very high heat. The shrimp will not be fully cooked. Sprinkle the salt and 1 tablespoon black pepper over the shrimp. Add the barbeque base and heavy cream and let the shrimp finish cooking, about 3 minutes more. Stir in the butter and serve with warm, buttered bread.

YIELD ~ 6 SERVINGS

SOURCING NOTES

An easy way to accumulate the shrimp shells for this recipe is to simply place shrimp shells into a plastic freezer bag anytime you make a recipe that requires peeled shrimp. Leave the bag in the freezer until ready to use. The shells will retain their flavor and last for months.

In Louisiana, everyone seems to have their own blend of Creole seasoning. Most contain a combination of paprika, garlic powder, onion powder, black pepper, cayenne, dried oregano, dried thyme, and dried basil. Use your favorite brand, or make your own.

KID-FRIENDLY COOKING

Let the kids help you make your own Creole seasoning. Have them taste each herb and spice and describe the flavor.

Let the kids lend a hand in cleaning the shrimp. Touching, smelling, and seeing the shrimp will evoke questions that touch upon subjects ranging from science to geography to cooking. Discuss where the shrimp are from, how they are harvested, what makes them pink. Every ingredient has a host of stories to tell.

Louisiana's wild shrimp is sustainable— it's the shrimper that's in jeopardy.

Cheap, imported, farm-raised shrimp is the biggest threat to our livelihood and even our health.

The imported product is loaded with chemicals and harvested in unsustainable ways. It drives down prices, and we just can't compete.

—Lance Nacio

Shrimp Boat on the Bayou 83

Chef John Besh
Louisiana Shrimp & Grits with Andouille

INGREDIENTS

FOR THE GRITS

- 4 cups water
- 1 teaspoon salt
- 1 cup Anson Mills stone-ground organic grits
- ½ cup mascarpone cheese
- 2 tablespoons unsalted butter

FOR THE SHRIMP & SAUCE

- 2 tablespoons olive oil
- 30 jumbo Louisiana shrimp
- 1 teaspoon Creole seasoning
- 1 teaspoon salt
- 6 tablespoons andouille sausage, *small dice*
- 1 tablespoon garlic, *minced*
- 1 tablespoon shallot, *minced*
- 2 tablespoons paquillo peppers, *small dice*
- 1 tablespoon thyme, *chopped*
- 30 ounces shrimp stock (See accompanying recipe.)
- 2 tablespoons unsalted butter
- 2 cups tomatoes, *diced*
- 1 tablespoon chives, *chopped*
- 1 teaspoon fresh lemon juice
- ½ cup fresh chervil for garnish

PREPARATION

For the Grits:

Bring the water to a boil and lightly season with the salt. Add the grits while stirring rapidly, and turn down to a simmer. Stir constantly, making sure to keep the grits from sticking to the bottom of the pot. Simmer the grits on low for about 20 minutes, stirring all the time. To finish, stir in the mascarpone cheese and butter.

For the Shrimp and Sauce:

In a large pan over medium temperature, heat the olive oil. Season the shrimp with Creole seasoning and salt. Sauté the shrimp until they begin to brown but are not cooked all the way through. Remove the shrimp and hold on the side. Add the andouille sausage, garlic, shallot, paquillo peppers, and thyme to the pan, and sauté until they become aromatic. Add the shrimp stock and bring to a low simmer. Stir in the butter and reduce the liquid until it becomes thick. Return the shrimp to the pan and cook through. Finish with the diced tomatoes, chives, and lemon juice.

ON THE PLATE

Place four tablespoons of the grits in the middle of a large bowl. Arrange the shrimp in the middle so they stand up (tails facing in), and spoon the sauce around to fill the negative space. Garnish with the fresh chervil.

YIELD ~ 6 SERVINGS

SOURCING NOTES

Chef Besh uses only Anson Mills grits. All of Anson Mills' products are hand-ground, which means that you get a creamier texture, without using loads of butter. Many of Anson Mills' grains utilize heirloom or ancient varieties. Anson Mills products are available in most supermarkets, or can be ordered online at ANSONMILLS.COM.

One of Chef Besh's favorite Louisianan purveyors is Jacob's World Famous Andouille. Andouille (pronounced "awn-doo-ee") is a smoked pork sausage that is seasoned with Cajun spices, cured, then smoked. To order from Jacob's World Famous Andouille, visit CAJUNSAUSAGE.COM.

Chef John Besh
Louisiana Shrimp Stock

PREPARATION
Simmer the celery, carrot, onion, thyme, garlic, and shrimp shells, covered in water, for 1 hour over low heat, skimming the fat the whole time. Strain and reserve.

INGREDIENTS
1 rib celery, *quartered*
1 large carrot, *peeled and quartered*
1 medium onion, *peeled and quartered*
1 sprig fresh thyme
1 head garlic, *split in half*
2 pounds shrimp shells
1 gallon water *(or just enough to cover)*

SOURCING NOTES
Any true Louisianan will tell you that the only crustaceans that could possibly be used for good Shrimp Stock or Shrimp & Grits are wild-caught Louisiana jumbo shrimp. Ask for Louisiana shrimp at your local grocer, or order online at LOUISIANASEAFOOD.COM.

Shrimp Boat on the Bayou

Chef John Besh
Tempura Gulf Shrimp with Hoisin Salad

INGREDIENTS

FOR THE TEMPURA SHRIMP
1 can (12 ounces) club soda
1 cup all-purpose flour
1 pinch salt
18 jumbo Louisiana shrimp
2 cups canola oil, *for frying*

FOR THE DIPPING SAUCE
1 cup fish sauce
1 cup rice wine vinegar
1 cup sugar
1 tablespoon chili paste

FOR THE SALAD
1 cup rice wine vinegar
1 cup olive oil
2 cups hoisin sauce
1 teaspoon shallot, *finely minced*
1 teaspoon garlic, *finely minced*
1 pound salad greens
Zest from 1 lime, *for garnish*

PREPARATION

FOR THE TEMPURA SHRIMP:

Stir together the club soda, flour, and salt until combined. Remove the veins from the shrimp and dip them into the club soda mixture.

Heat the canola oil in a heavy saucepan to 150° F. Carefully drop the shrimp, one at a time, into the oil and fry until golden brown, about 3 minutes.

FOR THE DIPPING SAUCE:

Combine the fish sauce, vinegar, sugar, and chili paste. Bring the sauce to a boil. Boil for 2 minutes, to combine the flavors. Set the sauce aside and let cool until serving.

FOR THE SALAD:

To make the hoisin vinaigrette, stir together the vinegar, olive oil, hoisin sauce, shallot, and garlic until well combined. Toss the greens with the hoisin vinaigrette.

ON THE PLATE

Place the tempura shrimp on a platter and serve the dipping sauce alongside. Garnish the plate with curls of lime zest.

YIELD ~ 6 SERVINGS

Cooking and eating with your children should be the focus of all families. We would solve a lot of problems in our society if families would just sit down, talk, and eat together.

–Chef John Besh

SLIPPERY BUSINESS ~
HOW TO PEEL A SHRIMP
Shrimp are less expensive per pound if you peel them yourself.

TO PEEL SHRIMP:
- Grasp the tail in one hand and the legs in the other. Break the legs away from the body.
- Peel back the shell, and remove it.
- With a sharp knife, make a shallow slit in the back of the shrimp from the tail to the front. Remove the dark "vein" (actually the intestine) in the center if you see one.
- Rinse in cold water.

STARS & STRIPES ~
CHOOSE AMERICAN SHRIMP
Most of the shrimp sold in the United States are imported from countries with less-rigorous standards for shrimp.

Imported wild shrimp most often are farm-raised. These farming practices often pollute the bays and estuaries where the shrimp are raised. To avoid disease among farmed shrimp, foreign shrimp farms use the antibiotic chloramphenicol, which has no safe level of human exposure, according to the U.S. Food and Drug Administration. Chloramphenicol is forbidden in U.S. shrimp farming. Foreign-farmed shrimp also may have been exposed to other pesticides and antibiotics in high volumes. Studies have found up to 21 pesticides and poisons—many banned in the United States—in a single bite of foreign, farm-raised shrimp!

Additionally, foreign-caught wild shrimp are often caught in trawling nets that trap large quantities of other sea life—called bycatch—that often are injured or killed in the process. These nets drag along the seafloor, harming the natural environment.

Regulations governing shrimping in U.S. waters require the use of catch-reduction devices as well as other safety mechanisms to ensure that the waters and fish species stay healthy.

- When buying shrimp, ask for wild-caught American shrimp to ensure that your product is safe and environmentally friendly.

EAT YOUR WORDS ~
EXPRESS YOURSELF OVER DINNER
Everyday speech is jam-packed with food metaphors, such as *"he's a shrimp," "fish for compliments," "flat as a flounder," "don't be chicken," "dropped like a hot potato."*

- As a topic for dinner conversation, see how many food-related expressions you can come up with.

SPICE THINGS UP ~
WHAT'S THE DIFFERENCE?
What makes a spice a spice, or an herb an herb? It's not as arbitrary as it seems. An herb is the green leaf or tender stem of a plant. It can be used fresh or dried. A spice is another part of the plant—seed, bark, flower, fruit, or root—and usually is used dried.

MEASURING UP ~
WHEN IS A CUP NOT A CUP?
One recipe calls for a cup of sliced onion, a second for a cup of diced onion, and a third for a cup of finely chopped onion. What do these terms mean?

- **SLICE:** Cut into thin sections.
- **DICE:** Cut into small cubes.
- **CHOP:** Cut into the smallest pieces possible.

- Does the technique make a difference in the size or the number of onions you need to fill a cup? Try it for yourself.

You should find that the smaller the pieces, the more onion you will need to fill the cup. A cup of chopped onion, for example, requires 50 percent more onion than a cup of sliced onion.

SHRIMP TALES ~
TEST YOUR UNDERWATER IQ

What color are raw shrimp?
- Pink
- Red
- Brown
- White

Answer: All of the above. Shrimp come in all four colors, depending on species.

What color are cooked shrimp?
- Pink
- Red
- Brown
- White

Answer: Cooked shrimp are usually pinkish in color. The pink color in wild shrimp comes from the brine and other seeea life the shrimp consume.

How many jumbo shrimp are in a pound?
- 16–20
- 21–25
- 26–30
- 31–35
- 36–40

Answer: There is no industry standard for shrimp designations such as "jumbo" or "large." Instead, shrimpers prefer to give the number of raw, unshelled shrimp per pound. On average, however, extra-jumbo shrimp have 16 to 20 per pound, jumbo shrimp have 21 to 25 per pound, extra-large have 26 to 30 per pound, large have 31 to 35 per pound, and medium have 36 to 40 per pound.

Where do shrimp grow up?
- Open ocean
- Wetlands
- Estuaries
- Coastline

Answer: Shrimp grow up in estuaries—places where rivers meet the sea and fresh and salt waters mix. Estuaries often are fringed by wetlands, such as swamps and salt marshes, where shrimp and many other fish and shellfish grow to adult size. The wetlands provide food and protection for the growing shrimp. Later in their lives, the shrimp move out to open water, where they swim in abundance.

Shrimp and prawns are the same animal.
- True or false?

Answer: The terms "shrimp" and "prawn" oftentimes are used interchangeably. Technically, however, shrimp and prawn are different species. There is one sure way to tell them apart: The side plates on a prawn's body all overlap. The shrimp's body is plated with one large middle section, making it appear more elongated.

What kind of animal is a shrimp?
- Reptile
- Fish
- Crustacean
- Mollusk

Answer: Crustacean. This is a group of animals that encompasses more than 52,000 species, including lobsters, crabs, crayfish, and shrimp. Like all arthropods, crustaceans have elongated, segmented bodies and jointed legs.

Where is a shrimp's skeleton?
- Inside
- Outside
- It doesn't have a skeleton.

Answer: A shrimp's skeleton is on the outside of its body. Shrimp, like all crustaceans, have a stiff exoskeleton, meaning the structural part is on the outside of the body and must be shed regularly to allow the animal to grow. Shrimp don't have a backbone like fish, so they are classified as invertebrates.

How much shrimp do Americans eat each year?
- 1 billion pounds
- 1.2 billion pounds
- 1.4 billion pounds
- 1.6 billion pounds

Answer: Americans eat 1.4 billion pounds of shrimp each year—around 2.5 pounds per person. That is more than the average amount of tuna we each consume. Only a small fraction of what we eat is wild U.S. shrimp. Most shrimp eaten in the United States comes from foreign shrimp farms. Wild American shrimp is now readily available, however, and is gaining in popularity.

Which state has the most productive shrimp industry?
- Louisiana
- Texas
- Mississippi
- North Carolina

Answer: Louisiana shrimpers land about 100 million pounds of shrimp annually, more than any other location in the United States. Louisiana shrimp are harvested year-round. Wild American shrimp also are harvested in Texas, Mississippi, Alabama, Florida, Georgia, North and South Carolina.

ACTIVITIES

PURE & SIMPLE ~
SEASONING FROM THE SEA

When ocean water is heated by the sun, it evaporates, leaving salt behind. Did you know that you can distill salt water by taking advantage of evaporation? Here's how:

WHAT YOU NEED
- Water
- Salt
- Large bowl
- Short glass or jar
- 2 small rocks (or other small weights)
- Plastic wrap
- Masking tape

WHAT YOU DO
- Add salt to 2 cups of tap water and stir until it dissolves. Pour into a large bowl.
- Place the jar in the middle of the bowl. Weigh it down by placing a small rock or weight inside.
- Cover the bowl with plastic wrap, using the masking tape to make sure you get a tight seal.
- Place a small rock or other weight on top of the plastic, directly over the glass in the bowl.
- Put the bowl outside in the sun. Leave it for several hours, or for the whole day. When you check it again, there will be water in the cup. Taste it to find out if the water is salty or fresh.

What happened? The sun warmed the water in the bowl until it evaporated, becoming a gas. When the gas rose and hit the plastic, it condensed and rolled down the plastic and into the glass (like rain falling from the sky). The salt was left behind in the bowl, making the water in the glass pure enough to drink. Now you have pure water to drink and salt to season your meal with.

- How do you think global warming could affect our seas? Does this experiment give you any clues? How do you think it could affect the marine life in shallow estuaries and wetlands?

SEA OF SURPRISES ~
LIFE IN THE ESTUARY

Wetlands and estuaries are filled with lots of different animals—from birds that stop in for a season on their way to somewhere else, to turtles, crabs, and other animals that spend their whole lives in the water.

You may be surprised to know that everyone in America lives near a wetland of some kind. It may be a creek, a river, a lake, a stream, an ocean, a marsh, or simply a water table.

- Look at a map and find some of the wetlands in your area. Visit a wetland and write down the names of as many creatures as you can see. (Be sure to look in the water, as well as on top.) How many kinds of creatures can you identify? Do you think there may be more creatures that you cannot see or that may visit during different seasons or times of day? Visit various wetlands in your area to see how they differ and what kinds of marine life exist in each location.

What we are fishin' for here in Louisiana comes from Mother Nature's pond.

–LANCE NACIO

LOST AT SEA ~
FIND YOUR WAY WITH A COMPASS
Boat captains and fishermen must rely on a compass and map to navigate the vast ocean. In the bayous of Louisiana, a compass is a vital tool for maneuvering through the ever-changing wetlands. You can make your own simple compass using household items. Us it to find your way the next time you are on the ocean—or maneuvering around the forest, a park, or your backyard.

WHAT YOU NEED
- Sewing needle
- Magnet
- Cork
- Nonmetallic bowl
- Water

WHAT YOU DO
- Rub the needle against the magnet several times, from the needle's eye to its tip.
- Stick the needle lengthwise through a thin piece of cork.
  (Use the top 1/8 inch of a wine cork, if you have one.)
- Set the cork and needle in a bowl of water. The needle should turn so that it faces in a north-south direction. If you have another compass, use it to check the accuracy of your magnetized needle.

Try making a portable version of your compass by using a smaller piece of cork and some water in a recycled paper cup. Take your compass to a park or outdoor area and test your skills:

- Stand so that your compass faces north.
- Mark off a square with sides 10 paces long: Mark the starting point, go 10 paces due north, then 10 to the east, 10 to the south, and 10 to the west, using sticks or rocks to mark the corners.
  Identify the direction of each corner.
- Use guidebooks to identify plants and animal tracks within each section of the square.
  What kinds of plant life do you see in the southern part of your square?
  What kinds are in the northern part of the square?
- In which direction is the sun? The moon? In which direction is the sun moving?
  In which direction is your shadow facing? In which direction are the birds flying?
- What other information can you gather from the direction of the sun?

ACTIVITIES

Fields, Not Feedlots

featuring

CHEF CATHAL ARMSTRONG
RESTAURANT EVE ALEXANDRIA, VIRGINIA
EAMONN'S: A DUBLIN CHIPPER ALEXANDRIA, VIRGINIA

JOEL SALATIN
POLYFACE FARM SWOOPE, VIRGINIA

"High priest of the pasture," reads a sign above the desk of farmer Joel Salatin, quoting what *The New York Times* recently called him.

The Washington Post wrote that Chef Cathal Armstrong "steps into another reality, using local ingredients … to produce dishes that are subtly, intriguingly unique."

The two connect when Chef Armstrong brings his children, Eve, age seven, and Eamonn, age four, to the rolling pastures of Joel Salatin's idyllic Polyface Farm.

Out amongst the cows, chickens, pigs, and rabbits, the family gets a lesson in where food really comes from.

They see how "pig power" builds the compost and happy chickens are left to express their "chickenness," wandering freely in Salatin's lush pastures.

From seeing day-old chicks to gathering eggs, from moving the cows to checking in on the very clean pigs, chef and children experience the circle of life on the farm in this culinary adventure.

Farmer Joel shows how his animals "do the real work"—fertilizing, aerating, composting—making clean food for the community without synthetic fertilizers, antibiotics, or other harmful chemicals.

Chef Armstrong then transforms the products of this "eco-agriculture" into mouth-watering dishes that nourish the palate and the soul.

Chef Cathal Armstrong
New World Braised Pork & Beans

INGREDIENTS

FOR THE PORK

1 gallon water
2 cups salt
1 cup white sugar
2 tablespoons pickling spice
8 cloves garlic
2 tablespoons whole black pepper
10 pounds pork belly, *skinned*
4 cups pork stock

FOR THE BEANS

2 tablespoons unsalted butter
½ teaspoon garlic, *minced*
1 tablespoon shallot, *minced*
1 cup fava beans, *blanched*
1 cup cipollini onions, *roasted*
2 cups braising liquid (*left over from the pork braising*)
1 cup cherry tomatoes, *halved*
1 tablespoon oregano, *chopped*
2 tablespoons basil, *chopped*
1 teaspoon thyme, *chopped*

PREPARATION

For the Pork:

Fill a large pot with water and add the salt, sugar, pickling spice, garlic, and pepper. Place in the refrigerator and let chill until cold. Place the pork belly in a nonreactive container and pour the chilled brine over it. Allow the meat to refrigerate for 4 days.

Remove the pork belly from the brine and cut into 8-ounce portions. Braise the pieces in the pork stock in a 275° F oven for 3 hours, or until fork-tender. Let cool completely in the liquid, then remove from the liquid. Place the pork in a hot pan over high heat. Sear each side of the pork until crisp.

For the Beans:

Sauté the garlic and shallot in ½ teaspoon of the butter until tender. Add the fava beans, onions, and braising liquid. Bring to a boil. Cook until the beans are tender. Remove from the heat. Add the remaining butter, and the tomatoes and herbs. Season to taste.

YIELD ~ 6 SERVINGS

KID-FRIENDLY COOKING

Oftentimes kids don't like things, simply because they don't know what they are or where they came from. Letting kids explore the story behind their food is a great way to get them interested in expanding their palette, and will help them make more informed food decisions in the future. Take the kids with you when you shop. Explain to them where their food comes from; that pork is from a pig and eggs are from chickens, cheese comes from milk and beef is from a cow, carrots grow in the ground and peaches come from a tree. Read the labels together so that you can decide what is important when making your food choices.

Why shouldn't the farmer be paid a fair wage?

People are willing to pay for their lawyers, their doctors, for their fancy cars.

Farmers are responsible for putting the food on your table and the fuel into your body.

Shouldn't we all be willing to pay a fair price for that? Shouldn't we all care about that?
—Joel Salatin

Chef Cathal Armstrong
Roasted Breast of Polyface Farm Chicken with Swiss Chard & Wild Virginia Chanterelles

INGREDIENTS

FOR THE SWISS CHARD
1 pound Swiss chard
2 tablespoons olive oil
2 tablespoons shallot, *finely minced*
½ tablespoon garlic, *minced*
Salt and pepper, *to taste*

FOR THE CHANTERELLES
2 tablespoons olive oil
½ pound chanterelle mushrooms, *cleaned*
2 tablespoons shallot, *minced*
½ tablespoon garlic, *minced*
1 teaspoon fresh thyme, *chopped*
Salt and pepper, *to taste*

FOR THE CHICKEN
1 tablespoon canola oil
4 chicken legs
4 chicken breasts, *butterflied*
1 tablespoon olive oil
1 tablespoon unsalted butter
12 cloves garlic
8 bay leaves
2 ounces malt vinegar
4 ounces chicken stock
2 ounces demi-glace
Salt and pepper, *to taste*

PREPARATION

FOR THE SWISS CHARD:
Heat a large cast-iron skillet until it is very hot. Add the olive oil, chard, shallot, garlic, salt and pepper. Stir-fry until just wilted, about 2 minutes. Place on a dry towel to absorb any excess liquid.

FOR THE CHANTERELLES:
Heat a large cast-iron skillet until it is very hot. Add the olive oil and mushrooms and sear until they are tender, about 2 minutes. Add the shallot, garlic, thyme, salt and pepper. Continue to cook for 1 minute more. Remove from the heat.

FOR THE CHICKEN:
Heat a large skillet over medium-high heat. Add the canola oil.

Season the chicken legs with salt and pepper. Place them in the skillet, turning occasionally. They will take about 10 to 12 minutes to cook, depending upon their size. After the legs have been in the pan for about 5 minutes, season the chicken breasts and add them to the pan. Cook, turning occasionally, until they are golden brown and cooked throughout. Remove the meat from the pan and let rest.

Wipe up the canola oil in the skillet. Add the olive oil, the butter, and the whole cloves of garlic. Sauté until golden, about 3 minutes. Deglaze the pan with the vinegar, and reduce until thick. Add the chicken stock, demi-glace, and bay leaves. Bring to a rapid simmer and reduce by half.

ON THE PLATE
Place the Swiss chard and chanterelles in a pretty arrangement on the plate. Place the chicken atop the vegetables. Garnish with the sautéed garlic. Drizzle the glaze over the top of the chicken. Season, to taste.

YIELD ~ 4 SERVINGS

SOURCING NOTES
Most family farms let their chickens run in wide-open spaces. Consequently, grass-fed chickens have a much richer taste and are much healthier for you. Their meat also cooks faster, because there is less fat. Look for local, sustainable, and grass-based farms from which to purchase meat and poultry products. Most farms offer fresh as well as frozen products, so the effort is worthwhile.

It's very important that we all know where our food comes from. The kids need to know the pork came from a pig, the baby chick grows up to be the chicken we cook with. We also need to know how those animals were treated, what they ate, how they were cared for.

–Chef Cathal Armstrong

WRIGGLE ROOM & RECYCLED EARTH ~
CREATING YOUR OWN COMPOST WITH WORMS

Composted soil has many nutrients and vitamins that help plants grow strong. Worms help create compost naturally. Worms are extremely helpful to plants, farmers, and the ecosystem in general. Their active tunneling not only aerates the soil, adding necessary oxygen, but also breaks down and spreads nutrients throughout the soil, making the ground fertile. You can create your own compost by recycling the things that you don't eat.

WHAT YOU DO
- Accumulate two days worth of food scraps for composting (banana and apple peels, bread crusts, tops of vegetables, coffee grounds, etc.). Using scissors, cut the materials into small pieces, no more than one-half inch in diameter.
- Get a plastic storage container, preferably about the size of a shoe box. Punch several holes in the lid of the container. The holes should be the size of a pencil or large nail head. Line the bottom of each container with small rocks or pebbles.
- Tear newspaper into strips and use them to create a 2-inch-deep layer on top of the rocks that are in your container. Sprinkle a 1-inch layer of garden soil on top. Add 1 to 2 tablespoons of alfalfa meal or other composting material from your garden store. Add a handful of food scraps on top. (If possible, try adding some coffee grounds as well to accelerate the process. Crushed Leaf clippings can also be added.)
- Roam the yard looking for worms or purchase several from your local garden or fishing store. Add a *small* handful of worms to the container, atop the food scraps. (You don't want to crowd the container.) Add another 1-inch-layer of garden soil on top of the worms. Sprinkle with several tablespoons of water.
- Cover the worm bin with the lid and place it in a cool location away from light. Add more food every few days, under the top layer of soil.
- Check back every few days to see how the decomposition is going. There should be a large increase in the number of worms and the food should be continually broken down by the composting and worms. Finished compost will be black and crumbly. Remove it with your hands or a spoon, taking care to leave behind as many worms as possible. You can continue to replenish the compost again and again, using it in your garden when needed and adding more food scraps as they accumulate.

Worms move an amazing amount of soil for their small size. An earthworm can eat its own weight in soil every day! Worms help till the soil as they tunnel through it. You can be sure some friendly earthworms will help get any compost you place in your garden down to the roots of your plants.

SOUS CHEF FOR A DAY ~
EVERYTHING IN ITS PLACE

In every restaurant, the *mise en place* is the center of any preparation. This staging of ingredients and utensils is called *mise en place*, literally translated as "everything in its place." Usually it is the job of the assistant, or sous, chef to prepare the *mise en place*.

Let the kids pitch in and be sous chefs for the day by measuring all of the ingredients and organizing the utensils, washing greens, peeling garlic and shallots, dunking mushrooms in water to clean them, and setting out measuring spoons. Place each item for the recipe in a small bowl or ramekin alongside the recipe. Having a *mise en place* makes it easy for kids to get involved in preparing any recipe—and it makes it easy for them to taste, touch, and smell each ingredient.

> **Agriculture is almost a lost art in this country. And It's sad, because there is nothing more beautiful and more rewarding than watching a family tend their farm.**
>
> –Chef Cathal Armstrong

LIFE OF THE SOIL ~
GETTING TO THE ROOT OF OUR FOOD

Few of us are directly involved in raising the food we eat. But the ingredients in any recipe, such as New World Braised Pork & Beans, can be traced back to the soil.

HERE'S HOW:
- pork ⇨ pig ⇨ corn & hay ⇨ soil
- beans ⇨ soil
- molasses ⇨ sugar cane ⇨ soil

※ What other ingredients in your kitchen can you trace back to the soil? Chart the paths of some of your favorite meals.

※ Plan a family visit to a local farm to see the roots of your food, first-hand. Ask a farmer at your farmers market if they offer tours or visits. When you visit a farm, you can see for yourself the many terrains, grasses, and soil types that contribute to our food system.

TURKEY TALK AND DOGGIE WALKS ~
DOMESTICATED ANIMALS COME TO AMERICA

Animals first were domesticated 9,000 to 10,000 years ago in the Old World. But in the New World, turkeys and dogs were the only domesticated animals until after Columbus' second voyage to the Americas.

※ What other animals are now domesticated? What are some of the animals we rely on most for our food? What animals can you think of that were domesticated for other purposes?

FUNGUS FEVER ~
MUSHROOM LOVE

Mushrooms are not plants, but fungi—organisms that get their energy from other organic materials. Instead of reproducing with seeds like plants, mushrooms reproduce through speck-like spores.

Many kinds of mushrooms used in cooking, such as button, shiitake, and chanterelle, have gills that contain the spores. The spores vary in size, color, and shape depending on the species of mushroom. You can use mushrooms purchased at the market to explore their differences and similarities.

WHAT YOU DO
※ Purchase several varieties of mushrooms. Make sure the cap is tightly closed against the stem. The gills are on the underside of the cap.
※ Remove the stems and place the mushrooms gill side down on white paper, leaving ample space between varieties.
※ Leave the mushrooms undisturbed in a draft-free place until the caps open and drop their spores onto the paper (usually a day or so).
※ Compare the colors, sizes, and patterns of the spores. How do they compare? Are there any unusual or surprising results?

ACTIVITIES

Hill Country Venison

featuring

CHEF DAVID BULL
DRISKILL GRILL AUSTIN, TEXAS

CHRIS HUGHES
BROKEN ARROW RANCH INGRAM, TEXAS

In Austin, Texas, there is a man named Bull who, contrary to his name, is no cowpoke—instead it's deer that strike his fancy, and fine dining is his game.

Recognized nationally as the next "rising star" of the culinary world, Chef David Bull ventures into the Texas Hill Country with his three sons for a lesson in biology and natural history.

They find themselves on Broken Arrow Ranch among clear-flowing streams, waterfalls, spectacular bluffs, and rocky vistas; there, they search for wild, exotic deer and antelope.

Chef and sons get up close to the majestic animals as they frolic through the craggy hills and plains of south Texas. And then the group sets out on a real-life search for the animals proclaimed by many to be "the most-prized meat on earth;" rare species of deer and exotic antelope.

Rancher Chris Hughes is the family's guide for this Texas safari in which wildlife abounds and conservation rules the land. It is a rare opportunity to see nature's wild side, up-close.

Chef David Bull
Slow-Cooked Wild Venison Stew

INGREDIENTS
1 pound venison stew meat, *large dice*
Salt and pepper, *to taste*
¼ cup all-purpose flour
2 tablespoons unsalted butter
2 tablespoons canola oil
¼ cup all-purpose flour
1 yellow onion, *small dice*
2 carrots, peeled, *small dice*
3 garlic cloves, *minced*
¼ cup poblano pepper, *small dice*
1 cup Shiner Bock beer
3 cups veal stock
1 cup potato, *peeled, small dice*
1 ear of corn, *shucked*

PREPARATION
Season the venison with salt and pepper, and dredge in flour. Shake off the excess flour. Heat a large sauce pot over medium heat. Add the butter and oil. Sear the venison in the butter-and-oil mixture until crisp and golden brown on all sides.

Add the onion, carrot, garlic, and poblano pepper to the pot. Add the Shiner Bock beer and bring to a boil. Add the veal stock and reduce to a simmer. Add the potato and corn, and cook for 1 to 1½ hours over low heat. Season with salt and pepper, to taste.

ON THE PLATE
Ladle 2 cups of the venison stew into each of 4 large dinner bowls.

YIELD ~ 4 SERVINGS

SOURCING NOTES
Shiner Bock is known as "the official beer of Texas." The rich, full-bodied flavor of this deep amber-colored beer gives the stew an authentic Texas taste. Rest assured, however, that you can use your own locally brewed amber beer in place of the Shiner Bock.

Broken Arrow Ranch's distinctive venison is the only kind that Chef Bull uses in his kitchen. Broken Arrow's methods keep the meat from tasting "gamey," and create a more tender bite. Broken Arrow ships across the United States—and its stew meat comes pre-diced for easy preparation. Order online at BROKENARROWRANCH.COM.

These animals are truly wild and free-range.

We are just here to manage the populations, to sustain the pasture and range lands ... to ensure the integrity of the land for the future.

—Chris Hughes

Hill Country Venison

Chef David Bull
Roasted Rack of Broken Arrow Venison with Grilled Trumpet Mushrooms

INGREDIENTS

FOR THE VENISON
1 "Chop Ready Rack" of venison, *preferably from Broken Arrow Ranch*
Salt and pepper, *to taste*
4 tablespoons canola oil

FOR THE MUSHROOMS
1 pound trumpet mushrooms, *split in half lengthwise*
4 tablespoons olive oil
Salt, *to taste*

FOR THE PRESENTATION
Freshly grated horseradish
Pea tendrils, *if desired*

PREPARATION

Preheat the oven to 375° F. Season the venison on all sides with salt and pepper. Heat a large sauté pan until very hot. Remove from the heat and add the canola oil. Place the pan back on the heat and sear the venison on all sides until golden brown and crisp, about 2 minutes. Place the rack of venison in the oven for 10 to 12 minutes, or until the desired degree of doneness is reached. NOTE: The venison rack will expand in size. Also, remember that the meat has very little fat and thus will cook much more quickly than beef. Remove the venison from the oven and let it rest.

Preheat an outdoor or wood-burning grill to 375° F. Coat the mushrooms in the olive oil and season with salt, to taste. Place the mushrooms on the preheated grill, flat side down, and grill for 2 minutes. Turn the mushrooms 45 degrees and grill for 2 more minutes. Reserve hot for assembly.

ON THE PLATE

Slice the venison rack into individual chops. Spread the Bacon Horseradish-Turnip Purée *(see accompanying recipe)* around the center of each of 4 large dinner plates, forming a circle on each plate. Place 4 to 5 pieces of the grilled mushrooms on top of the purée, slightly off-center. Crisscross 2 of the venison chops on top of the mushrooms and garnish with freshly grated horseradish and pea tendrils. Serve immediately.

YIELD ~ 8 SERVINGS

SOURCING NOTES

Broken Arrow Ranch sells "Chop Ready Racks" from both venison and antelope (larger cut of meat). Chef Bull prefers the Axis venison for this recipe; however, either would work well. The Axis Chop Ready Rack consists of 9 rib bones that can be cut into 8 individual chops, if desired. Order online at BROKENARROWRANCH.COM.

Chef David Bull
Bacon Horseradish-Turnip Purée

PREPARATION

Place the turnips in a large sauce pot. Cover them with water. Season the water with salt and bring to a boil. When the water is boiling, reduce the heat to a simmer. Continue to cook over medium heat until the turnips are soft and fork-tender. Strain the turnips and place in a high-speed blender. Add the butter and purée until smooth. Add the rendered bacon and the horseradish and mix until completely incorporated. Season with salt, to taste, and reserve hot for assembly.

YIELD ~ 8 SERVINGS

INGREDIENTS

2 pounds turnips, *cleaned, peeled and quartered*

Water, *as needed*

Salt, *to taste*

2 tablespoons butter

½ pound smoked bacon, *diced and rendered*

3 tablespoons prepared horseradish

Chef David Bull
Seared Venison Loin with Blackberry-Fig Jam & Braised Romaine

INGREDIENTS

FOR THE VENISON
1 pound venison loin, *trimmed*
Salt and pepper, *to taste*
2 tablespoons canola oil

FOR THE BLACKBERRY-FIG JAM
1 cup blackberries, *cut in half*
1 cup Black Mission figs, *quartered*
3 tablespoons sugar
3 tablespoons red wine vinegar

FOR THE BRAISED ROMAINE
1 heart of romaine lettuce, *cut into strips*
1 tablespoon unsalted butter
Lemon juice, *to taste*
Salt, *to taste*
Sunflower sprouts, *as needed for garnish*

PREPARATION

FOR THE VENISON:
In a large sauté pan over high heat, add the canola oil and sear the venison loin for 3 to 5 minutes on each side until a rare-medium rare doneness is achieved. Add half of the jam *(see instructions below)* to the pan and glaze the loin on all sides. Remove from the heat and allow to rest for 5 to 8 minutes.

FOR THE BLACKBERRY-FIG JAM:
Place the blackberries, figs, sugar, and vinegar in a small pot. Bring to a boil. Reduce the heat to low and simmer for 5 minutes. Remove from the heat and allow to cool. Place the mixture in a blender and purée until smooth. Reserve warm for assembly.

FOR THE BRAISED ROMAINE:
Place the butter in a large sauté pan over medium heat. Add the romaine lettuce and sauté for 30 to 40 seconds. Season with salt and lemon juice, to taste. Serve immediately.

ON THE PLATE
Using a pastry brush, brush the blackberry-fig jam across 4 dinner plates. Place the braised romaine in a line, slightly off-center. Slice the seared loin in even pieces and place the slices, overlapping, over the romaine. Garnish the plate with sunflower sprouts, if desired.

YIELD ~ 4 SERVINGS

SOURCING NOTES
Try experimenting with various kinds of fruit and berries in this recipe. Raspberries, strawberries, rhubarb, or even apples can be used in place of the blackberries. The sweetness of the jam offsets the subtle, sweet earthiness of the venison, however, so be sure to use fruits on the sweeter, not more acidic, spectrum.

KID-FRIENDLY COOKING
Purchase inexpensive paintbrushes from your local hardware store. Let the kids each create their own work of art by "painting" the jam on each plate. This technique can be used with any dish that involves a heavy sauce.

Chefs and farmers share a mutual respect for the environment—taking care of the land and the animals, respecting the ingredients, and always working toward sustainability.

–Chef David Bull

Hill Country Venison

DEER ME! ~
THE BACKYARD DETECTIVE

Deer have become inhabitants of many suburban neighborhoods. Because deer usually feed from dusk to dawn, you may not have seen one. But there are lots of animals that roam our yards, even if we live in an urban neighborhood.

Some creatures may even leave their tracks or hoof- prints in your lawn or flower beds. Look for their tracks. If you find them, you can easily make a cast of their prints.

WHAT YOU NEED
- Tin can with both ends cut out (coat inside with vegetable oil, if desired)
- Paper cup or bowl
- Plaster of Paris (available at craft stores)
- Water
- Popsicle stick (for mixing plaster)

WHAT YOU DO
- Locate a track with clean features present. Look in damp or sandy areas where the soil is soft.
- Being careful not to alter the track imprint, or to remove any debris or loose soil from the track.
- Place the open tin can over the track and press it lightly into the soil to seal it. Use a can that surrounds the entire track.
- In a paper cup or bowl, mix ¼ to ½ cup plaster of paris with water, using the popsicle stick. Mix until the consistency is similar to that of pancake batter.
- Pour the plaster into the can, covering the track and filling the can to a depth of about 1 inch.
- Let the plaster dry at for least 1 hour before moving the can.
- At home, let the plaster dry completely, for 24 hours.
- Remove the plaster cast from the can. (Coating the inside of the can with vegetable oil will make it easier to slide the cast out.)

Compare and contrast various casts. What kinds of animals are in your yard? Do they vary in size? Are they more plentiful in one season or another? Is there a particular plant or area of your yard that they seem to like best? Perhaps there is something in that area that is especially tasty!

LIFE UNDERGROUND ~
THE COLORFUL WORLD GROWING BELOW

Like turnips, many of our most familiar and nutritious vegetables grow underground. They include potatoes, carrots, beets, radishes, yams, parsnips, celery root, and red onions. Many are colorful, but none of them are green. That's because they don't contain chlorophyll, a pigment that is produced by plant structures that are exposed to sunlight.

- Make a list of your favorite green vegetables. How does each grow—on a tree, from a plant, in a bush, in a pod, from a flower? Chances are that each of them gets a good dose of sunshine each day.

- Make a list of your favorite colored vegetables. Do all of them grow underground? Do they have characteristics in common? Are there any clues that let you know whether they're grown above ground or below? Visit your local market and see if you can guess how each plant grows.

"LETTUCE" EAT ~
GREEN GODDESSES MAKE A STATEMENT

Take a trip to the market, and see how many different kinds of lettuce you can find. There are five basic types of lettuce:

- **CRISPHEAD:** This type of lettuce has a tightly clustered head and crisp leaves. It includes varieties such as iceberg.
- **LEAF:** Also called loose-leaf, this type produces crisp leaves loosely arranged around the stalk. This is the most common type of lettuce available. The leaves can vary from green to shades of red. Varieties include oak leaf, ruby, and black-seeded Simpson.
- **BUTTERHEAD:** The butterhead varieties are generally small and loose–headed, with tender, soft leaves.
- **ROMAINE:** Romaine, or cos, lettuce produces long, upright leaves formed in a loose head.
- **STEM:** These varieties form an enlarged seed stalk that is used mainly in cooked dishes. Their robust stems usually require heating or stewing. There are many Asian varieties, as well as chard and kale, in this family.

Low in calories, lettuce is an excellent source of vitamin A. Lettuces are also easy to grow in your garden or in a hanging pot.

SHOOTING FOR THE TOP ~
GROW YOUR OWN GARNISH
The shoots of snap and snow peas make unusual garnishes that are easy to grow in your garden. The shoots—the top 2-to 6-inch tips of a young pea plant—include tender leaves and immature tendrils. The shoots have a light, refreshing pea pod flavor and can be used raw as a garnish or in a salad. They can also be lightly sautéed in sesame oil or steamed as an Asian-style vegetable. Pea shoots may be small, but they are packed with vitamins A, C, and K.

× To grow pea shoots and tendrils, sow seeds in the garden in early spring, as soon as the soil has warmed to 40° F—or try them indoors in a sunny window. When plants are 6 to 8 inches tall, clip off half of the shoot. You should be able to harvest new shoots about once a month.

You may have other garnishes already growing in your garden. Edible flowers include pansies and other members of the violet family, nasturtiums, and roses. Squash blossoms and herb flowers are also popular choices. Of course, do not ever use any flower that has had a pesticide applied to it!

PAINT THE TOWN RED ~
SAUCY DESIGNS FOR YOUR PLATE
Add artistic flourish to a dish that calls for a sauce or a glaze.

× Pick up a variety of paintbrushes, in all sizes, at your local hardware or crafts store. Give each diner a plate, a small cup to hold the sauce or glaze, and a choice of brushes.

Let the diners be their own decorators, brushing the sauce on their plates to create their own designs. Plate the meat or fish atop the sauce. You will have a table full of artistic work to show off at dinner!

ACTIVITIES

Winter Bay Scallops

featuring

CHEF MICHEL NISCHAN
THE DRESSING ROOM—A HOMEGROWN RESTAURANT
WESTPORT, CONNECTICUT

ROD TAYLOR
TAYLOR BAY SCALLOPS FAIRHAVEN, MASSACHUSETTS

What are celebrity chef Michel Nischan and his two sons doing in a small boat off the coast of Cape Cod on a windy five degree day on which ice is blocking their passage?

Nischan believes in pure and simple food selection, in which produce is eaten in season and no food is injected with hormones, pesticides, or "any of that funny stuff."

Chef Nischan is so dedicated to this ethic that the frozen waters of Buzzards Bay will not deter him.

With waterman Rod Taylor as their captain, the chef and his sons brave the ice for one of nature's perfect offerings: the bay scallop, with its pink and orange shell and translucent, sweet meat.

Breaking the ice, the group pulls up Taylor's sweet specialty: in-shell scallops that taste of green apples and the sea.

Chef Michel Nischan
Taylor Bay Scallop Farrotto

INGREDIENTS
2 tablespoons grapeseed oil
2 tablespoons shallot, *chopped*
1 cup butternut squash,
    roasted and cut into small dice
1 cup fava beans,
    peeled and cooked
1 cup mushrooms, *cooked*
6 cups farro, *cooked*
2 ¼ cups vegetable stock
3 tablespoons mascarpone cheese,
    at room temperature
Sea salt, *to taste*
¼ cup butternut squash purée
2 tablespoons farm-fresh milk
Freshly sliced herbs
Salt and pepper, *to taste*

SOURCING NOTES
Farro is an heirloom variety of spelt wheat, commonly used in Italy. Today, it can be found in gourmet and specialty stores, as well as in most Whole Foods Markets. As in this dish, farro is often used as a substitute for risotto because of its hearty quality. Anson Mills produces an heirloom variety of farro that is extra firm in texture, making it ideal for this recipe.

PREPARATION
Heat 1 tablespoon of the grapeseed oil in a medium sauce pot over medium heat. Add the shallot and cook, stirring constantly, until shallot turns soft and transparent, about 1 minute. Add the squash, fava beans, and mushrooms to the mixture. Sauté until heated through. Add the farro and 1¼ cups of the vegetable stock to the mixture. Bring to a simmer and cook until all of the liquid is absorbed. Remove the mixture from the stove.

Add the mascarpone and gently stir, until the cheese is well incorporated.

Meanwhile, shuck the scallops over a small bowl fitted with a strainer so that you capture the scallop juice as you shuck. Fold all of the scallop juice into the *farrotto* mixture.

Heat a large sauté pan over high heat until hot. Add the remaining 1 tablespoon of grapeseed oil to the pan, then immediately add the scallops.

Sauté the scallops, tossing continually, until they are nicely browned, about 3 to 5 minutes. Lightly sprinkle with the sea salt and transfer to a warm platter. Set aside.

In a separate small sauce pot, heat the remaining ¼ cup of vegetable stock, mixed with the squash pureé. Remove from the heat.

Add the milk to the vegetable stock and squash mixture and whip with a battery powered cappuccino foamer.

ON THE PLATE
Divide the *farrotto* equally among 6 small bowls. Divide the scallops over each serving. Spoon the foam on top of the scallops and sprinkle with freshly sliced herbs. Add salt and pepper, to taste.
    YIELD ~ 4 SERVINGS

To get the very best, you have to know the people who grow, catch, or raise the food. And they have to do it with love, respect, and dignity.

–Chef Michel Nischan

Winter Bay Scallops

Chef Michel Nischan
Green Apple Sweet Scallop Lollipops

INGREDIENTS

FOR THE SCALLOPS

1 egg, *lightly beaten*
2 tablespoons water
20 bay scallops, *shucked and cleaned*
½ cup spelt flour
½ cup bread crumbs
1 quart grapeseed oil
20 bamboo skewers

FOR THE DRESSING

1 tablespoon local apple cider
1 tablespoon apple cider vinegar
1 tablespoon local honey
2 teaspoons grain mustard
¼ cup grapeseed oil
2 tablespoons of your favorite fresh herbs, *lightly chopped*
Salt and pepper, *to taste*

FOR THE SALAD

4 cups assorted salad greens
1 small red beet, *scrubbed, roasted, and sliced thin*
1 small yellow beet, *scrubbed, roasted, and sliced thin*
1 locally grown apple, *cut into quarters, with seeds removed*

PREPARATION

FOR THE SCALLOPS:
Whisk the egg and water together until thoroughly blended.

Place the scallops in the spelt flour and toss until lightly coated. Shake the excess flour off the scallops, dip them briefly in the beaten-egg mixture, and then place in the bread crumbs to coat well.

Place the grapeseed oil in a pot small enough that the oil fills it halfway. Heat the oil to 350° F. Drop the scallops into the oil and fry until lightly browned, 2 to 3 minutes. Transfer the scallops to a dish lined with a few layers of paper towel. Insert a skewer into each of the scallops and keep warm.

FOR THE DRESSING:
Combine the cider, cider vinegar, honey, and mustard in a small bowl. Whisk thoroughly to combine. While whisking, slowly add in the ¼ cup grapeseed oil. Finish by stirring in the herbs, then season to taste with salt and pepper.

FOR THE SALAD:
Place the salad greens and beets in a medium mixing bowl and toss well with a few tablespoons of the apple dressing.

ON THE PLATE

Place an apple quarter on one side of each of 4 salad plates. Insert 5 scallop "lollipops" into each apple wedge. Divide the salad equally among the 4 plates and mound next to the apple wedges with the scallop skewers. Drizzle the plates with extra dressing, if desired.

YIELD ~ 4 SERVINGS

SOURCING NOTES

Seek out sustainable and kid-friendly seafood. Many seafood choices today contain high levels of toxins and pollutants, including mercury. Other species are severely over-fished and their populations threatened. Bay scallops are considered a "kid-safe" seafood. To find other seafood choices that are both sustainable and kid-friendly, visit KIDSAFESEAFOOD.ORG.

It's about finding food with a story, it's about getting the whole family involved—It's about choosing foods that are healthful and will actually promote the health of your children. Food brings families—brings people—together in so many wonderful ways.

–Chef Michel Nischan

Winter Bay Scallops 115

BLOWIN' IN THE WIND ~
THE SCALLOPS CHIME IN

For much of human history, shells have been used for money, utensils, jewelry, and even musical instruments. Scallop shells can be turned into a garden wind chime.

WHAT YOU NEED
- Scissors
- Thin nylon beading thread
- At least 6 clean scallop shells, hinges intact
- Plastic coffee-can lid
- Paper clip or fastener

WHAT YOU DO
- Cut 1-foot lengths of beading thread—one for each scallop shell.
- With a slip knot, tie the thread around the shell hinge. Tighten the slip knot so that the thread extends from the middle of the hinge.
- In a circle around the coffee-can lid, ½ inch from the edge of the lid, poke as many evenly spaced holes as there are shells. Use a hole punch or pin to create the holes.
- Thread the end of each string (with shell attached on opposite end) through each of the holes you placed in the lid. Tie the free end of each thread to a paper clip or fastener, so that the string cannot slip through the holes. Each shell should hang from the lid.
- Poke one additional hole in the center of the lid. Put the free end of a thread through the hole from the underside of the lid and tie to a paper clip. Use the paperclip to hang your chime from a hook outdoors.

RING-A-DING ~ APPLE RINGS

You can make dried apples to eat as a snack or to turn into a necklace. It's a great way to eat your apples all year long—and you know what the doctor says about an apple a day!

WHAT YOU NEED
- 4 apples
- Knife
- 1 teaspoon lemon juice
- 3 tablespoons water
- Sturdy thread or twine

WHAT YOU DO
- Cut the apples into rings about 1/8 inch thick.
- Mix the lemon juice and water in a shallow dish. To prevent discoloring, dip each apple ring into the lemon-water mixture.
- String the thread or twine through the center of each ring and hang in a dry, warm place. The rings will take about 2 weeks to dry.

When dry, the rings will have a chewy texture. Drying apples helps to preserve their sweetness and nutrients. These dried apple rings make a healthy snack for school or any time of day.

You can also use the Apple Rings as decorative elements to a Fall table. Why not use them as fun, edible napkin rings?

"FAR-OUT" FARRO ~ AN ANCIENT COMEBACK

Farro is Italian for spelt, a grain in the wheat family. It is one of the oldest grains—first cultivated around 7,000 years ago, at the beginning of agriculture. Spelt is one of a number of ancient grains, among them quinoa and amaranth, that are being rediscovered by contemporary cooks.

These "forgotten" grains tend to be higher in protein, fiber, and other nutrients than more familiar grains such as wheat and rice. Cooking with these new-old grains is a novel way to add whole grains to your diet.

When you can get fresh, delicious, sustainable seafood—and you get it into your kids' hands and they pop it in their mouths—have their taste buds fire off and their brains start working … it's the most amazing thing in the world.

It's good for them, it's good for the environment—you get them to make that connection when they are young. It's just awesome.

–Chef Michel Nischan

MOLLUSK MUSTS ~ FRESH IS BEST

Scallops, clams, oysters, and mussels should be alive when they are cooked or when they are opened to eat raw. How can you tell if a mollusk is alive? The shell should be tightly closed. If it's not, tap on it. If the shell closes, the animal is alive and using its muscle to close the shell. If the shell stays open, the animal is dead and should not be eaten. And never eat any shellfish that does not open its shell when cooked.

COME ON, JOIN THE BAND ~ SCALLOP SHAKERS

A scallop has two identical, mirror-image shells. As a defense against predators, the scallop can tightly close its shell, using its muscle to swim and hide.

Scallop shells come in beautiful hues of pink, green, purple, and blue. You can make a beautiful and fun musical instrument using leftover scallop shells.

- Take two identical scallop shells.
- Place one shell down, with the inside of the shell facing up. Place a small handful of uncooked rice in the shell.
- Line the outside edge of the shell with glue. (Use a heavy glue such as super glue.)
- Carefully place the other scallop shell on top, making sure that the edges meet.
- Let your shell dry overnight.

You now have a beautiful, one-of-a-kind musical instrument. Scallop shakers also make great place-card holders for a party. Simply write the name of the guest on the scallop shell, using paint or an art pen. Place one shaker at each person's plate.

' ON THIN ICE ~ WHY DON'T OCEANS FREEZE?

Have you ever wondered why rivers and lakes freeze in the winter, but oceans never fully freeze solid?

WHAT YOU NEED
- Gallon-size freezer bag
- Crushed ice
- Salt
- Thermometer
- Quart-size freezer bag
- Water

WHAT YOU DO
- Fill the gallon-size freezer bag halfway with crushed ice. Add 1 cup of salt and seal the bag.
- Put on some gloves and knead the ice and salt until the ice has completely melted. Use the thermometer to record the temperature of the salt-water mixture. When the ice has melted, the temperature should be less than freezing (which is 32˚F or 0˚C).
- Now put about an ounce of water in the quart-size freezer bag. Seal the quart bag and then put it in the salt-water mixture in the larger bag. Seal the larger bag also, and leave it until the water inside the quart bag freezes.

What happened? Could you make the salt water freeze solid? Salt always lowers the freezing point of water, because its compounds break up the molecular structure of water. The more salt in the water, the lower the temperature needed to make it freeze.

On our adventure to harvest scallops off of Cape Cod, the shallow waters in the bay were nearly frozen solid. Why did those waters freeze while the deeper waters didn't? Can you imagine being a scallop in that cold water?

ACTIVITIES

New York Dairy

featuring

CHEF BILL TELEPAN
TELEPAN RESTAURANT NEW YORK, NEW YORK

RON OSOFSKY
RONNYBROOK FARM ANCRAMDALE, NEW YORK

Chef Bill Telepan garners reviews that rave about the "clarity and focus of his food... elegant and without gimmickry."

The New York Times commends his cuisine for "...its freshness, pureness and punch of flavors; the pure skill with which it's been cooked." So it is no surprise that trips to the farm happen regularly for this young chef.

Accompanied by his daughter Leah, as he often is, Chef Telepan heads out on a milking adventure with farmer Ron Osofsky of Ronnybrook Farm in upstate New York.

"Hopelessly out of date, and proud of it," says Ron while milking and making milk products the way his family has for three generations: in small batches, delivered at peak freshness, gently pasteurized, and hormone-free.

From milking Elvis the cow to churning fresh ice cream, there's plenty to do on this dairy farm, and the whole family lends a hand.

Chef and daughter chase the cows and help milk the herd on a frigid winter day—all in pursuit of the perfect glass of milk. And in this case, that comes served warm, straight from the cow.

Chef Bill Telepan
Mixed Beet Salad with Fresh Buttermilk & Chive Dressing

INGREDIENTS

FOR THE SALAD

4 bunches fresh baby beets, *trimmed; your choice of Chioggia, golden, red, striped, or other beets that are in season*
2 tablespoons olive oil
4 tablespoons water
Kosher salt, *to taste*

FOR THE DRESSING

2 ounces farm-fresh buttermilk
2 tablespoons lemon juice
2 tablespoons fresh chives, *thinly sliced*
2 tablespoons olive oil

PREPARATION

Preheat the oven to 450° F. Place the beets in foil with the olive oil and 4 tablespoons of water. Sprinkle the beets with salt. Fold the foil to seal them in. Place the beets in the oven on a baking sheet (to catch any escaping juices or water). Roast until they're tender and easily pierced with a knife, about 25 to 30 minutes. Set aside to cool.

Mix together all of the ingredients for the buttermilk dressing.

When the beets are cool, peel them by rubbing with a towel. Slice the beets in half.

ON THE PLATE

Place the beets on a plate and drizzle with dressing. Garnish with greens or herbs. Serve immediately.

YIELD ~ 4 APPETIZER PORTIONS

SOURCING NOTES

Seek out farm-fresh milk at your local farmers market or grocery store. Fresh milk products have a satisfying taste that is especially accentuated in simple recipes like this. And farm-fresh dairy products generally contain more vitamins and nutrients than ultra-pasteurized and commodity dairy products.

Instead of buttermilk, you can use fresh, plain yogurt. The results are just as delicious and a bit easier for the kids to dive into.

KID-FRIENDLY COOKING

Chioggia or candy-stripe, beets have brightly colored stripes that make them appear whimsical and as appealing as candy. The bright colors are perfect for tempting kids! And they make a beautiful presentation for parties.

This recipe is easy for the kids to make: They can use kid-safe scissors to cut the chives, mix the dressing with a small whisk or fork, and peel the cooled beets by hand. For added fun, let the kids plate the salad themselves and get creative with the presentation.

Ronnybrook is the type of farm I like to be involved with.

They're a family farm that loves what they are doing— and it shows.

You can always tell when someone loves what they are doing, whether it's a chef or a farmer—it really comes out in the quality of the food.

–Chef Bill Telepan

New York Dairy 121

Our milk tastes a lot different than most milk you drink. We process it much more slowly than conventional operations; the cows are treated well and they eat mostly grass, all year 'round. You can just taste the difference.

—Ron Osofsky

Chef Bill Telepan
Cauliflower with Egg Noodles, Farmer's Cheese & Black Pepper

PREPARATION

Cut out the core of the cauliflower and break into large florets. Then cut out the cores of the individual florets to make even smaller florets. (You'll want small, bite-size pieces.)

Melt 2 tablespoons of the butter in a large sauté pan, over high heat. When the butter begins to bubble and brown, add the florets. Spread them over the entire surface of the pan and cook for 3 minutes, tossing only 1 time about halfway through, so the florets brown well.

When they're well browned, add the water or stock and remaining butter to the pan and cook an additional 3 minutes, or until the cauliflower begins to get tender, but is still a little crunchy. (The small florets will finish cooking as you add the pasta and cheese.)

Bring a pot of lightly salted water to a boil and cook the fettuccine until tender (2 to 3 minutes for fresh pasta, 8 to 10 minutes for dried pasta). Drain.

Mix the farmer's cheese and pepper together in a bowl, making sure that the cheese is crumbly.

Add the fettuccine to the pan with the cauliflower. Reduce the heat to low. Toss the fettuccine, butter, and cauliflower mixture until the cauliflower is distributed throughout. Toss in the cheese-pepper mixture. Season with salt.

ON THE PLATE

Place a generous portion on each of 4 plates. Top with additional pepper and cheese, if desired. Serve immediately (although this dish also makes an excellent cold pasta dish, too).

YIELD ~ 4 SERVINGS

INGREDIENTS

- 1 small head cauliflower, *cut into florets*
- 4 tablespoons butter
- 1 cup water, or vegetable or chicken stock
- 1 pound fresh egg fettuccine
- 12 ounces farmer's cheese
- 1 teaspoon freshly ground black pepper
- Salt, *to taste*

SOURCING NOTES

To bring color to this recipe, combine a number of cauliflower varieties, in different colors. Look for whatever varieties grow best in your area.

KID-FRIENDLY COOKING

Let the kids break off the cauliflower florets by hand, crumble the cheese, and toss the pasta. The fun cauliflower colors will make everyone forget that they are eating a vegetable!

It is important to cook with your children. Being together, having conversations, and teaching them to cook... It's a great way to learn about each other.

—CHEF BILL TELEPAN

Chef Bill Telepan
Leah's Favorite "Vanilla Pudding Sundae Surprise" with Caramelized Oranges & Cookies

PREPARATION

For the Pudding:
Mix the sugar, flour, and salt together in a bowl.

Combine the milk and vanilla (pods and scrapings) in a pot and cook over medium heat, until simmering. Add the flour mix. Whisk the ingredients together and cook on low heat for 5 minutes, whisking constantly.

Pour a few tablespoons of the hot milk mixture into a bowl with the egg yolks, to temper. Pour the yolks into the pot, and whisk constantly for 10 minutes, until thick. Remove the vanilla bean pods. Whisk in the butter until combined. Cover with plastic wrap. Let sit for at least 30 minutes.

For the Caramelized Oranges:
Segment the oranges and place in a small bowl. Place the sugar and 2 ounces of water in a small pot. Cook on medium heat until they're combined and the color turns to amber. Add the orange juice, ½ cinnamon stick, and salt, and reduce until slightly thick, about 5 minutes more. Pour over the oranges and let cool, or let sit overnight in the refrigerator.

ON THE PLATE
Crush the vanilla and/or chocolate cookies until crumbly.

Place the pudding in dessert bowls or martini glasses, layering it with the cookie crumbs, and oranges. Serve immediately.

YIELD ~ 4 SERVINGS

KID-FRIENDLY COOKING
Let the older kids do the work of stirring and stirring and stirring the pudding. Just be sure to stay close at hand to keep them from burning themselves.

The smell and essence of fresh vanilla bean can be an awakening for kids, who are used to artificial scents and flavors. Let them handle the bean, smelling it and guessing what's inside. Then let them scrape the inside of the pod, using a butter knife.

Create a dessert bar, with cups full of cookie crumbs, fruit, and pudding. Let each kid—and adult—create their own perfect sundae.

INGREDIENTS

FOR THE PUDDING
1 cup sugar
¼ cup flour
½ teaspoon salt
2 cups whole milk
1½ vanilla beans, *scraped, pods and scrapings reserved*
4 egg yolks
4 tablespoons unsalted butter

FOR THE ORANGES
4 medium oranges, *peeled*
1 cup sugar
2 ounces water
2 ounces fresh orange juice
½ cinnamon stick
Pinch of salt

FOR GARNISH
Vanilla and/or chocolate cookies

If you pay attention to the seasons... you'll find the best products.

–Chef Bill Telepan

SHAKE IT UP ~
HOMEMADE BUTTER

It's remarkably easy to make your own butter. It just takes a bit of shaking. All you need is heavy cream and a jar with a tight-fitting lid.

- Fill a glass jar halfway with heavy cream. Screw the lid on tightly.
- Shake vigorously for about 10 minutes until the cream solidifies.
- Pour off the liquid, which is buttermilk.
- Add salt to the butter, if you like.
- Store the butter in the refrigerator as it is, or press it into a decorative mold or cookie cutter.

Grandma probably made butter in a similar fashion, hand-churning the milk until it was thick and ready to eat.

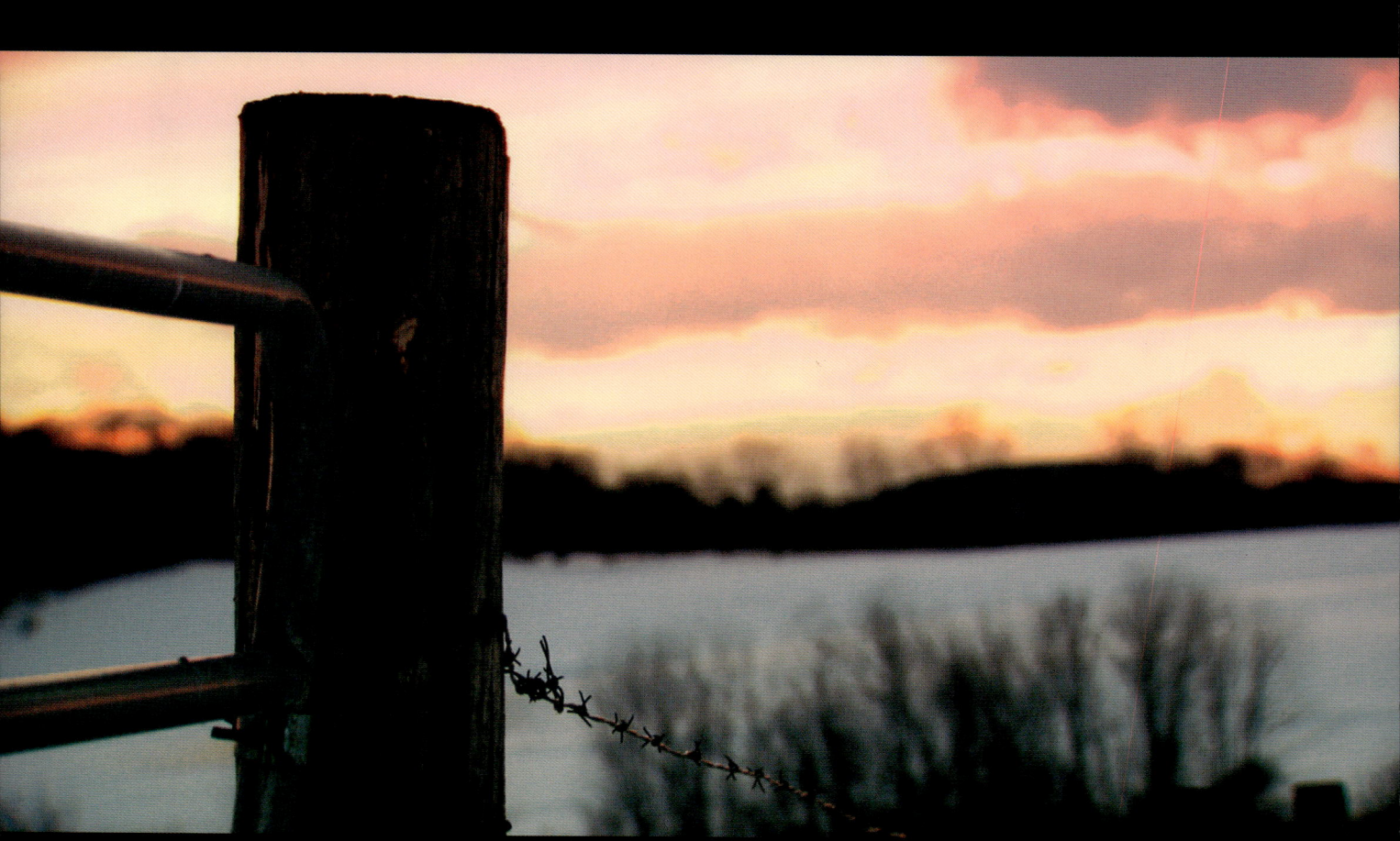

UDDERLY COOL ~ COW IQ

At New York's Ronnybrook Farm, the cows roam the pastures freely, foraging on grasses and hay. At Ronnybrook, the family raises and milks the cows, churns the butter, bottles the milk, and whips the ice cream in much the same way as they have for generations. See if you know as much about cows as they do at Ronnybrook Farm.

How many pounds of whole milk do you need to make one gallon of ice cream?
- 1 pound
- 4 pounds
- 8 pounds
- 12 pounds

Answer: It takes 12 pounds of whole milk to make one gallon (128 ounces) of ice cream.

How much whole milk do you need to make one pound of butter?
- 5.3 pounds
- 10.6 pounds
- 21.2 pounds
- 42.4 pounds

Answer: You need the cream from 21.2 pounds of whole milk to make a pound of butter.

How much does the average dairy cow at Ronnybrook Farm weigh?
- 700 pounds
- 1,400 pounds
- 2,100 pounds
- 2,800 pounds

Answer: The average dairy cow weighs 1,400 pounds—equivalent to about nine average adult women.

How much milk does a free-range dairy cow produce in a day, on average?
- 13 pounds
- 33 pounds
- 53 pounds
- 73 pounds

Answer: A mature cow at Ronnybrook Farm produces about 53 pounds of milk each day—about 6.2 gallons.

Cows have a great sense of smell. How far away can they smell an odor?
- 2 miles
- 4 miles
- 6 miles
- 8 miles

Answer: A cow can smell you 6 miles away—long before you can smell her!

How much water does a cow need to drink each day to make that much milk?
- 35 gallons
- 25 gallons
- 15 gallons
- 10 gallons

Answer: 35 gallons—about a bathtub-full.

When you milk a cow, how many squirts make a gallon of milk?
- 410–420
- 340–350
- 270–280
- 200–210

Answer: When hand-milking a cow, it takes 340 to 350 squirts to fill a gallon bucket, so each squirt contains about ¾ tablespoon of milk.

In 2004 (the most recent year for which statistics are available), what portion of money spent on food eaten at home went toward dairy products?
- 11 percent
- 14 percent
- 16 percent
- 17 percent

Answer: Only 11.2 percent of the money that people spent at the grocery store went toward dairy products; 13.9 percent went for cereal and baked goods, 16.4 percent for meats and poultry, 17.3 percent for fruits and vegetables.

SMOOTH OPERATOR ~
THE TRICK TO TEMPERING EGGS

Adding a hot liquid to beaten eggs is tricky. If the liquid is added too fast, the eggs will scramble and form lumps. To avoid this, add about a quarter of the hot liquid to the eggs, which will warm but not scramble them. Then the egg-liquid mixture can be safely stirred with the remaining hot liquid. Try adding hot milk to eggs all at once and see what happens.

MILK MAIDS ~ HOW TO MILK A MATRON?

Ever wonder how to milk a cow? All you need is a low stool, a bucket, two hands—and, of course, a cow.

- Sit on the stool along the right flank of the cow so that you can reach the cow's teats.
- Wash the teats with a clean cloth and warm, soapy water.
- Place a stainless-steel milking bucket under the teat to be milked.
- Grasp the teat (closest to the bag, or udder) in the palm of your hand. Squeeze at the top of the teat between the thumb and forefinger. Close the next finger and then the next until you get to your pinkie, forcing out the milk with each squeeze.
- Release the teat, and repeat until only a small amount of milk comes out and the udder is soft. As you become more accomplished, you can milk with 2 hands at once.

FROZEN FANTASIA ~ WHAT'S IN YOUR CONE?

When it comes to frozen desserts, what's the difference?

- **ICE CREAM** is made from cream, milk, sweetener, flavoring, and sometimes eggs. Commercial ice cream must contain at least 10 percent milk fat to be called ice cream.
- **SHERBET** is a mixture of sweetened fruit juice or purée and water. It can also contain milk, egg whites, and/or gelatin.
- **SORBET** is like sherbet but never contains milk.
- **FROZEN CUSTARD** is similar to ice cream but is made with eggs in addition to cream and sugar.
- **SOFT SERVE** is generally lower in fat than ice cream and is dispensed from a machine instead of being served by hand.
- **GELATO** is an Italian ice cream made from milk and sugar. Gelato is stirred instead of whipped, resulting in a denser texture.

A BETTER BEAN ~ PODS OF PLENTY

Vanilla is America's favorite ice cream flavor. But many of us think of vanilla as simply "plain" ice cream. Vanilla, however, is an ancient ingredient.

Vanilla comes from the pod of the vanilla orchid, *Vanilla planifolia*, a vine native to Central America. Vanilla most often is used as a liquid extract that has been made from crushed vanilla beans steeped in ethyl alcohol and water for several days. Much of what is sold as vanilla extract, however, is not real vanilla. Instead, it is a synthetic form of vanillin, the main flavoring component of the vanilla bean's seeds and pod.

You can also extract flavor from the vanilla pod by burying it in granulated sugar.

- Place a vanilla pod in 2 cups of sugar, seal tightly, and let sit for 1 to 2 weeks.

The subtle flavor of the vanilla sugar is good in coffee, milk, and whipped cream, or added to fresh fruits. Try making hot chocolate using plain sugar and vanilla sugar. Can you taste the difference?

> *Commercial milk has been so adulterated, it really doesn't taste like milk anymore.*
>
> –RON OSOFSKY

I SCREAM, YOU SCREAM ~
WE ALL SCREAM FOR ICE CREAM

After hundreds of years, the best ice creams still are made with fairly simple ingredients: milk, cream, sugar, and sometimes eggs. Homemade ice cream is fun and easy to make in any weather. Here's how to make your own single-serving ice cream:

WHAT YOU NEED
- ½ cup milk
- ½ cup cream (which is higher in fat than milk)
- ¼ cup sugar
- ½ teaspoon vanilla or other flavoring
- Quart-size freezer bag
- 2 cups crushed ice
- ½ cup salt (rock or table)
- Gallon-size freezer bag

WHAT YOU DO
- Stir the milk, cream, sugar, and vanilla or other flavoring together in a bowl.
- Pour the mixture into the quart-size freezer bag.
- Place the crushed ice and salt in the gallon-size freezer bag.
- Place the quart-size bag inside the gallon bag.
- Begin shaking the bags so that the ice cream ingredients are whipped together. Make sure that the ice-salt mixture is evenly distributed throughout the larger bag.
- When the ice cream is thick, remove from the bag and enjoy!

Why add salt? Salt lowers the freezing point of water, which causes the ice to melt at a lower temperature. The lower freezing point provides the temperature difference needed to transfer heat between the freezing ice cream ingredients and the melting ice. Rock salt does not lower the freezing point as much as table salt does. (It results in smoother ice cream, because it freezes more gradually.)

ACTIVITIES

Wild Foraging & Island Duck Eggs

featuring

CHEF JASON WILSON
CRUSH SEATTLE, WASHINGTON

JEREMY FABER
FORAGED & FOUND EDIBLES SEATTLE, WASHINGTON

CHERRY MORGAN
MORGAN'S ROOST VASHON ISLAND, WASHINGTON

Forsooth, fair friend, would you like to forage in the forest?

Chef Jason Wilson has become the wonder boy of the Seattle food scene, stealing the spotlight from the region's old guard to reign as the new face of Northwest cuisine.

In true Seattle style, Chef Wilson straps on his boots to trek deep into the woods around Puget Sound in search of maple blossoms, fiddlehead ferns, stinging nettles, fragrant berries, and an assortment of other exotic offerings from the forest, with friend and forager Jeremy Faber. Through the forests surrounding Seattle, they gather wild ingredients of unlikely appeal.

Then Chef Wilson jumps aboard a ferry for a ride to Vashon Island, where his mother-in-law farms rare breeds of island duck and chickens for their eggs. Here, they see the workings of the family farm, chase some ducks, and gather eggs for the restaurant.

With his young son in tow, Chef Wilson embarks on a true culinary adventure amidst the forests, waters, and islands of the Pacific Northwest.

People always look at me and say, 'What you do is so weird. How do you eat that stuff?'

But to me, this isn't weird—this is what we are supposed to eat.

This is how our ancestors survived.

—Jeremy Faber

Chef Jason Wilson
Brioche French Toast with Maple Blossoms & Salmonberry Flower Cream

PREPARATION

For the Brioche French Toast:
Bring the 2 cups of cream and the Armagnac to a simmer. Add the sugar and maple blossoms to the mixture. Let simmer for approximately 10 minutes; avoid letting the cream mixture boil. Add the thyme. Pour the mixture into a blender and purée.

Strain the mixture. Pour it into a mixing bowl or baking pan. Beat the eggs. Add the eggs to the cream mixture. Place the slices of brioche into the mixture and allow them to soak for 10 minutes on each side.

In a sauté pan on medium heat, add the butter, then the slices of bread; brown the bread on both sides and place in a preheated 350° F oven for 5 minutes.

For the Salmonberry Flower Cream:
Bring the vanilla (insides/pod seeds) to a simmer with the 1½ cups of cream and the ¼ cup of sugar in a stainless-steel sauce pot on medium heat. Simmer for 5 minutes to infuse the cream with the vanilla. Whisk together well and let cool.

Chop the salmonberry flowers until fine and fold into the cream. Whip the mixture by hand until the cream thickens and forms a stiff peak.

ON THE PLATE
While the browned bread is still warm, divide brioche between two plates. Top each slice with the Salmonberry Flower Cream.

YIELD ~ 2 SERVINGS

INGREDIENTS

FOR THE FRENCH TOAST
2 cups heavy cream
¼ cup Armagnac
¼ cup white sugar
3 cups maple blossoms, *fresh, crushed*
1 teaspoon thyme, *chopped*
4 farm eggs
4 slices brioche, *1" thick*
2 tablespoons butter, *melted*

FOR THE SALMONBERRY FLOWER CREAM
1 vanilla pod, *split, with insides removed and reserved*
1½ cups heavy cream
¼ cup white sugar
1 cup fresh salmonberry flowers

SOURCING NOTES
Chef Wilson uses locally foraged salmonberry flowers and maple blossoms in this recipe, as they are readily available in the Pacific Northwest. Try using whatever is availablein your region. Use lavender, mint, rosemary, or other herbs as a substitute for the maple blossoms. In place of the salmonberry flowers, you can use other herbs, edible flowers, or a few ripe berries.

If you decide to forage on your own, always consult a professional as well as reference materials. Many areas have local experts and information that can assist you with choosing safe products: Try consulting your local community college, university, parks department, or culinary organization, or a reputable regional field guide.

Chef Jason Wilson
Wild Watercress Hollandaise

INGREDIENTS

3 cups watercress, *washed; preferably wild*
4 farm-fresh chicken eggs
1 tablespoon Sherry vinegar
1 tablespoon kosher salt
½ cup extra virgin olive oil
2 tablespoons butter, *melted*

SOURCING NOTES
Be cautious when sourcing watercress from the wild. It is vital that the water source be pristine and free of any toxins or poisons. It is best to leave foraging to an expert, especially if young children will be eating the meal.

PREPARATION
In a heavy 2-quart saucepan, bring heavily salted water to a boil.

Add the watercress and blanch for 30 seconds. Remove and immediately place in an ice-water bath for 1 minute. Gently squeeze out the excess water and place in a blender.

On high speed, purée the watercress and all of the other ingredients, until smooth.

ON THE PLATE
Pour a generous serving of hollandaise over Dungeness Crab & Wild Nettle Gratin. *(See accompanying recipe.)* Serve warm.

> *The people that we serve understand what sustainable, local foods are. They love to hear the stories about where their food comes from and what's in season, what's fresh from the farm or forests, today.*
>
> —Chef Jason Wilson

KID-FRIENDLY COOKING
Sometimes the best part of cooking doesn't happen in the kitchen. Take the kids on an expedition to discover what kinds of edibles are right in your own backyard. Take along a reputable field guide or expert if you plan to eat what you forage. Be sure to caution the kids that they should never pick or eat anything wild without consulting a parent or expert first. Many items can be toxic.

Wild Foraging & Island Duck Eggs **135**

I had so much fun in the forest and gathering eggs at grandma's farm.

My son got to see all these things for the first time. It was a great experience for both of us.

—Chef Jason Wilson

Chef Jason Wilson
Dungeness Crab & Wild Nettle Gratin with Grandma's Poached Duck Eggs

PREPARATION
In a stainless-steel sauce pot, blanch the nettles in highly salted boiling water for 1 minute. **NOTE**: *Use tongs or garden gloves to pick up the nettles! They will sting you if you touch them with bare hands.*

Arrest the cooking by shocking the nettles in highly salted ice water for 1 minute. Remove the blanched nettles. Bundle them in a clean towel and wring them out till nearly dry. Chop the nettles, being sure to squeeze out as much water as possible. Reserve the nettles.

Combine the duck fat and cream in a small, heavy pot. Add the leeks, garlic, thyme, and lemon zest to the fat-and-cream mixture, and simmer until reduced by half. Remove from the heat.

Add the salt to the mixture. Fold the nettles and crabmeat into the liquid. Place the warm mixture in a casserole dish or *cazuela* (earthenware dish) and top with the breadcrumbs.

Bake in a preheated oven at 400° F for 20 minutes, or until bubbly. Allow to rest for 5 minutes.

Poach the eggs to your liking.

ON THE PLATE
Place a generous scoop of gratin on each plate. Top with a poached farm-fresh duck or chicken egg and with Watercress Hollandaise. *(See accompanying recipe.)* Serve immediately.

This dish is not only an exceptional breakfast or brunch dish, but a perfect and exotic first course for dinner or lunch. Or try placing the gratin atop your favorite greens for a hearty main-course salad.

YIELD ~ 4 SERVINGS

INGREDIENTS
- 2 pounds fresh stinging nettles, *leaves only*
- ½ cup clean duck fat
- ½ cup heavy cream
- 2 leeks, *sliced in rings ¼ inch thick and soaked in warm water*
- 2 cloves garlic
- 1/3 bunch fresh thyme, *sprigs removed, chopped fine*
- 2 tablespoons lemon zest, *chopped*
- 2 tablespoons sea salt
- 2 pounds Dungeness crabmeat
- ½ cup brioche breadcrumbs, *lightly toasted, crusts removed*
- 4 duck or chicken eggs, *poached*

SOURCING NOTES
Wild nettles sometimes can be found at local farm markets and specialty stores. But remember that when handling them, you must wear protective gloves or use tongs, to avoid being stung. Once the nettles are cooked, their sting disappears.

If stinging nettles are not available, you can easily substitute spinach or even fresh chard. The exotic and interesting flavor of the nettles, however, is well worth the extra effort. And nettles are packed full of vitamins and nutrients.

EAT IT UP! ~
PARTS OF A PLANT WE EAT
What do the seed, leaf, stem, and root of a plant have in common? The parts of the plant we eat may be all of these—it all depends on the plant and the cuisine.

- Take a trip to the produce section of your market. Select ingredients for a recipe that includes each plant part we eat: leaf, root, stem, seeds. For example, make cole slaw with cabbage (leaf), carrot (root), celery (stem), and cashews (seeds).

QUACK, QUACK ~
NOT ALL EGGS ARE CREATED EQUAL
CHICKEN EGGS ARE THE MOST POPULAR EGGS FOR SUNDAY morning breakfasts and afternoon quiches in America. But there are lots of foul that provide eggs commonly found in supermarkets and farm markets: duck, quail, even ostrich.

	DUCK EGG	CHICKEN EGG
CALORIES	185	149
PROTEIN	12.8 grams	12.5 grams
TOTAL FAT	13.8 grams	10.0 grams
IRON	3.9 milligrams	1.4 milligrams
VITAMIN A	1,329 IU	635 IU

Amounts indicated are per 100 grams of edible portion. IU stands for "international unit."

DID YOU KNOW?
- A hen requires 24 to 26 hours to produce an egg. Thirty minutes later, she starts all over again.
- The egg shell may have as many as 17,000 tiny pores over its surface. Through them, the egg can absorb flavors and odors.
- Eggs age more in one day at room temperature than in one week in the refrigerator.
- If an egg is accidentally dropped on the floor, sprinkle it heavily with salt for easy cleanup.
- Egg yolks are one of the few foods that naturally contain vitamin D.
- For the first three to six months of laying, hens often will produce very small eggs, about one-third the size of a normal egg.

TAKE A SPIN ~
HOW TO TELL IF IT'S HARD-BOILED
Do you know how to tell a hard-boiled egg from a raw one without cracking it open?

- With them resting on their sides, spin a raw and a hard-boiled egg on a hard, flat surface. With a fingertip, stop the eggs from spinning and release them.

The raw egg will start to spin again. Why? Because of inertia: The liquid inside the raw egg continues to move and starts the egg spinning again. Inertia is what makes you continue to move forward in a car when it stops suddenly.

"EGGSPERT" ADVICE ~ KEEP IT COOL
Farm-fresh eggs usually are superior to supermarket eggs in their taste and texture. Regardless of where eggs are purchased, however, keeping eggs cold is key to maintaining their freshness.

At room temperature, eggs "age" rapidly—they can age more in a single day than in a week in the refrigerator. As an egg ages, its white and yolk lose quality: The white thins and loses some of its leavening power; the yolk gets flatter and larger and is more easily broken.

TO MAINTAIN MAXIMUM FRESHNESS:
- Store eggs in their carton to retain moisture and keep out odors.
- Keep eggs in the main refrigerator compartment instead of in the bins on the refrigerator door, since the door is a warm spot in the refrigerator.
- If a recipe calls for eggs at room temperature, cover them for a minute or two in hot water. They will come to room temperature quickly.

TRY THIS:
- Leave an egg at room temperature for one day and compare it to a refrigerated egg from the same dozen. Crack open both eggs and compare the appearance of the whites and yolks. What differences do you see? Do they smell or look different? Discard the unrefrigerated egg.

"EGGCELLENT" FACTS:

Scrub-A-dub-Dub:
Should You Wash Eggs?
No. Government regulations require that USDA-graded eggs be carefully washed and sanitized using a special detergent. Then the eggs are coated with a tasteless, natural mineral oil to protect them. (A freshly laid egg has a natural protective coating.)

Tick-Tock:
Why Do Cooked Eggs Spoil Faster Than Fresh Eggs?
When an egg is hard cooked in the shell, the protective coating is washed away, leaving bare the pores in the shell, and making it possible for bacteria to enter and contaminate the egg. Hard-cooked eggs should be refrigerated within two hours of cooking and used within a week.

Cracking Up:
What Makes Hard-Cooked Eggs Hard to Peel?
The fresher the egg, the more difficult it is to peel after hard boiling. That's because the air cell, found at the large end of the shell between the shell membranes, increases in size the longer the raw egg is stored. As the contents of the egg contract and the air cell enlarges, the shell becomes easier to peel. For this reason, older eggs make better candidates for hard cooking.

WHICH CAME FIRST? ~
WHY NOT ALL CHICKENS ARE CREATED EQUAL

"Pastured" is the name given to chickens that are allowed the freedom to roam and that are raised outside in the open air, on natural grasses and feed. Many commercial chickens today, however, are caged, are unable to walk or roam, and are fed hormones and antibiotics to make them produce eggs more quickly and cheaply.

Pasture-raised chickens obviously have a healthier and happier life, but what about their eggs? Laboratory testing found that, compared to the USDA standards, *pastured* and *free-range* chicken eggs contained:

- 34 percent less cholesterol
- 10 percent less fat
- 40 percent more vitamin A
- Twice as much omega-6 fatty acid
- Four times as much omega-3 fatty acid
  (*Source:* USDA)

For more research related to pastured livestock and other sustainable farming methods, check out:
- sare.org
- eatwild.com
- polyfacefarm.com

ACTIVITIES

ON THE TIP OF MY TONGUE ~
TASTE TEST TO TEMPT YOUR PALETTE
We can taste five flavors:
- Sweet
- Sour
- Bitter
- Salty
- Umami (best described as savory)

Contrary to what you may have heard, we sense all tastes, to varying degrees, on all parts of our tongues. We also can detect more than one flavor at one time, so we often combine different tastes in a recipe.

※ Taste as many foods from this list as you can, or make up your own list. Which taste would you assign to each? Do some have more than one taste?

※ Combine ingredients to create a "salad of tastes." Choose an ingredient from each of the five flavor categories and combine the ingredients in a salad.

apples	watercress
mushrooms	pecans
walnuts	spinach
radishes	oranges
curly endive	romaine lettuce
pine nuts	strawberries
green grapes	red bell pepper
avocado	goat cheese

FOREST IN A JAR ~
GROW YOUR OWN RAIN FOREST
A forager relies on Mother Nature for his harvest, gathering ingredients from forests and woodlands. You can create your own indoor rain forest or terrarium.

To make your own terrarium, you will need a large glass or plastic jar that has a lid. Poke a few small holes in the lid. Cover the bottom of the jar with 2 to 3 inches of dirt. Plant various plants in the jar and seal with the lid.

Small shade- and water-loving plants are the best kinds for terrariums. Try planting some of these varieties in your jar: Venus flytraps, ferns, mosses, ivy, chamomile, begonias, cyclamen, African violets, orchids.

You will need to water your plants only very occasionally, if at all. The water vapor from the plants will stay in the terrarium and be "recycled" continually. The terrarium has a moist, rain forest-like environment.

There is so much wild food available all around us—there for the taking—right at our doorsteps.

—Jeremy Faber

TWEET- TWEET ~
MAKE A BACKYARD BIRD & BUTTERFLY FEEDER

Birds and butterflies help spread pollen and seeds in your yard. Keep track of the various kinds of birds in your neighborhood by creating your own bird feeder.

WHAT YOU NEED
- Water
- Sugar
- Hammer and nail
- Small jar (such as a baby food jar)
- kitchen sponge
- String
- Construction paper or artificial flowers

WHAT YOU DO
- Make some food for your feeder with nine parts water and one part sugar mixed together. Add the sugar to the water and boil in a pan until it is dissolved. Let it cool.
- Use a nail and a hammer to punch a small hole in the lid of the jar. Cut a strip of the kitchen sponge and pull it through the hole in the lid, leaving about 1/2 inch sticking out from the top of the lid. You want the sponge to be a tight fit—it should get soaked with the sugar water, but not drip.
- Next, tie some string around the mouth of the jar. Cut two more lengths of string about 30 inches long. Take one and tie an end to the string around the mouth of the jar. Attach the other end on the opposite side of the jar to make a loop. Tie the second length of string in the same way to make a second loop perpendicular to the first one. Use one more piece of string to tie the tops of the loops together. Now turn the jar upside down and make sure it hangs steadily.
- Decorate the jar with brightly colored construction paper (flower shapes are best) or artificial flowers. The "prettier" it is, the more it will attract butterflies!
- Fill the jar with the cooled sugar water, screw the lid on tightly, and turn the jar upside down. Hang your feeder outside and wait for the butterflies to come!

WHIPPED INTO SHAPE ~
THE CHANGING FACE OF AN EGG

The success of a soufflé depends on beating egg whites until they form stiff peaks.

TO MAKE A SOUFFLÉ, YOU NEED:
- Egg whites at room temperature
- Egg whites free of any yolk
- A very clean bowl, free of any fats
- A small source of acid (vinegar, lemon juice, or a copper bowl)

You can test these for yourself to see which give you the biggest souffle.

WHAT YOU NEED
- Egg white at room temperature
- Egg white fresh from the refrigerator
- Egg white at room temperature with a bit of yolk in it
- Egg white at room temperature with acid added

WHAT YOU DO
- Beat each egg white in a separate bowl until stiff peaks form. (The white with the yolk may never form stiff peaks.)
- Compare the volume of each of the four beaten egg whites, using a glass measuring cup.
- Which beaten egg white has the greatest volume? Why do egg whites increase in volume when they're beaten?

The action of beating the egg white causes the proteins (albumin) to form bubbles, much like agitating soapy water creates bubbles.

ACTIVITIES

Resources & Ideas for Sustainable Living

including

SUPPORTING SUSTAINABILITY
- SUPPORTING LOCAL FAMILY FARMS
- WHAT CAN YOU DO?
- SHOPPING WITH AN ENVIRONMENTAL MIND
- ALL ABOUT ORGANIC
- PRODUCE SELECTION & STORAGE TIPS
- CLEAN & GREEN
- SUSTAINABLE SEAFOOD

PEOPLE & PLACES
- CHEFS & RESTAURANTS
- FARMERS, FISHERMEN, RANCHERS & GROWERS
- MORE INFORMATION AND RESOURCES
- THE SPONSORS
- THE PRODUCERS

All of us can and should aspire to appreciate, to the depths of our soul, the aesthetic pleasures surrounding food grown and prepared with integrity.

...Our relationship with food forms a tapestry into which each of us weaves a portion of the landscape our children will inherit, one bite at a time.

—Joel Salatin

Supporting Local Family Farms ...

WHY ARE FAMILY FARMS IMPORTANT?

The dramatic expansion of industrial, factory farmed agriculture has made it difficult for small family farmers in the U.S to stay in business.

Family farmers are being forced out of business at an alarming rate. According to Farm Aid, every week 330 family farmers leave their land. As a result, there are now nearly five million fewer farms in the U.S. than there were in the 1930's.

In addition to producing fresh, nutritious, high-quality foods, small family farms provide a wealth of benefits for their local communities and regions.

COMMUNITY: Family farms support their communities and serve as responsible stewards of the local land. By living on or near their farms, they have an interest in preserving the surrounding environment and community for future generations.

GREEN SPACES: The existence of family farms guarantees the preservation of green space within the community. Unfortunately, once a family farm is forced out of business, the farmland is often sold for development, and the quality land and soil for farming are lost.

LOCAL JOBS AND ECONOMY: Independent family farms also play a vital role in rural economies. In addition to providing jobs to local people, family farmers also help support small businesses by purchasing (and providing) goods and services within their communities. Family farme help preserve an essential connection between consumers, their food, and the land upon which this food is produced.

SAFETY: The loss of small family farms has also reduced our supply of safe, fresh, sustainably-grown foods and it is eliminating an important aspect of our national heritage. If we lose our family farmers, we'll lose the diversity in our food supply, and what we eat will be dictated to us by a few large corporations or overseas regulations.

WHY BUY LOCAL?

Most produce in the US is picked 4 to 7 days before being placed on supermarket shelves, and is shipped for an average of 1500 miles before being sold. And this is when taking into account only US grown products! Those distances are substantially longer when we take into consideration produce imported from Mexico, Asia, Canada, South America, and other places.

Cheap energy and agricultural subsidies facilitate a type of agriculture that is destroying and polluting our soils and water, weakening our communities, and concentrating wealth and power into a few hands. It is also threatening the security of our food systems, as demonstrated by the continued e-Coli, GMO-contamination, and other health scares that are often seen nowadays on the news.

We can start now by buying locally grown food whenever possible. By doing so you'll be helping preserve the environment, and you'll be strengthening your community by investing your food dollar close to home. Only 18 cents of every dollar, when buying at a large supermarket, go to the grower. 82 cents go to various unnecessary middlemen. Cut them out of the picture and buy your food directly from your local farmer.

TO FIND A FARMER OR PURCHASE LOCALLY GROWN FOOD, VISIT
LOCALHARVEST.ORG
SARE.ORG
WHOLEFOODS.COM

DID YOU KNOW?

- According to the EPA, 3,000 acres of productive U.S. farmland are lost to development every day.
- Between 1974 and 2002, the number of corporate-owned U.S. farms increased by more than 46 percent.
- 85% of Americans trust smaller scale family farms to produce safe, nutritious food.
- In the US, the average principal farm operator is 55.3 years old.
- Between 2005 and 2006, the US lost 8,900 family farms (more than 1 farm per hour).

WHAT CAN YOU DO?

If you care about how your food is produced, learn about and become an active participant in the food system. As a customer, your food-buying dollars become your clout, and where you choose to spend those dollars your vote for or against food production methods.

FARMERS MARKETS provide an opportunity for eaters to meet and talk directly with the people who grow their food. Farmers, too, can learn more about their customers.

COMMUNITY AND SCHOOL GARDENS can provide an important source of fresh produce, particularly for under-served populations in low-income neighborhoods. They are also good sources of information about growing food, as well as places for community gatherings.

COMMUNITY SUPPORTED AGRICULTURE (CSA) farms allow people to buy shares in the harvest of a farm before the crops are planted. In exchange for their investment, "shareholders" receive fresh fruits and vegetables (and sometimes products such as cheese, flowers, eggs and meat), weekly throughout the season. CSA members accept part of the financial risks associated with farming and enjoy access to "their" farms for educational events and volunteer opportunities.

PICK-YOUR-OWN FARMS AND ROADSIDE STANDS provide access to fresh produce directly from the farmer who grew it. Prices of pick-your-own are reduced in exchange for your labor, and the trip to the farm provides an excellent outing for groups of families and friends, particularly children.

BUYING ORGANIC PRODUCTS supports farmers who do not use chemical pesticides or fertilizers and who adhere to federal standards to protect the environment. Organic products provide premium prices to producers for their extra management, time, and risk. Look for "certified organic" labels when shopping.

TALK TO THE SOURCE OF YOUR FOOD to learn more about how it is grown. Join and patronize food co-ops, ask grocery managers to buy from growers and processors who use sustainable methods, and ask for food origins on restaurant menus. If you express interest in eating sustainably produced and processed food, chances are that your suppliers will respond.

SEEK OUT ALTERNATIVE SOURCES for buying other products such as cheese, honey and meat. Most areas have local producers that raise livestock using free-range and grass-based strategies. Find locally produced meats at your farmers market or supermarket.

Shopping with an Environmental Mind ...

Disposable or recyclable? Styrofoam, plastic or paper? Organic? Non-toxic? Today, millions of people are concerned about the environment. While complicated issues such as global warming, forest preservation and toxic waste may be too much for one person to solve alone, it is easy for consumers to make a difference by incorporating simple changes and conscious choices during routine activities such as shopping.

Every choice – from supporting a local farmer to buying products in recycled packaging, reusing durable items to purchasing an energy efficient appliance – extends the opportunity to do the right thing by choosing to use fewer of the Earth's precious resources. Shopping with an environmental mind means considering every step a product undergoes from its source to your home, everything from packaging to processing, humane animal treatment to product testing.

Next time you're filling your grocery cart, keep some of these simple ideas in mind as a way to do your part.

BUY LOCAL PRODUCE AND FOODS. Locally grown food is fresh, delicious, and it supports farm families in your community. Visit local farmer's markets to meet the folks who grow your food. A well-managed family farm is a place where resources—such as fertile soil and water—are valued.

BUY ORGANIC PRODUCE AND PRODUCTS. it is the best method for promoting sustainable agriculture and protecting the environment and the farm workers.

REDUCE, REUSE, RECYCLE. It is easy to do by reducing the amount of items you discard, reusing containers and products, and recycling as much as possible, including buying goods made with recycled content to "close the loop," creating a market for items recycled curbside or in other recycling programs.

ASK FOR NATURAL MEATS AND POULTRY. Ask your grocer for products without artificial ingredients, minimally processed, and raised humanely without the use of artificial growth hormones, antibiotics or animal by-products in their feed. Natural meat tastes delicious!

MAKE THE BEST ENVIRONMENTAL CHOICES WHEN PURCHASING SEAFOOD. At the same time seafood is touted as a healthy food source, the majority of the world's marine stocks are fully fished, over exploited, depleted or recovering at a slow rate. Whether purchasing wild caught or farm-raised fish and seafood, ask if it comes from a reputable, environmentally sound source. Your choices make a difference!

PURCHASE FOODS IN BULK. From a tablespoon of sunflower seeds to 50 pounds of whole wheat flour, buying in bulk reduces unnecessary product packaging and allows consumers to choose as much—or as little—of an item, thereby preventing spoilage or waste.

HAPPY COWS, DELICIOUS MILK PRODUCTS. The best bet to find milk and dairy products free of antibiotics and growth hormones is to choose organic, which requires animals to be humanely treated with access to the outdoors and fresh air, clean water and organically grown feed.

MINIMIZE USE OF DISPOSABLE GOODS. Purchasing reusable or refillable products decreases waste. Consider purchasing refillable razors, rechargeable batteries, refillable pens and even toothbrushes with replaceable heads. Think durability!

SELECT EGGS LAID BY HENS THAT ARE HUMANELY TREATED, including those labeled "free range," "free roaming," or "uncaged." Also, eggs marked as "fertile" means the eggs are laid by hens able to freely roam and mate with roosters.

CHOOSE EARTH-FRIENDLY HOUSEHOLD CLEANERS—OR MAKE YOUR OWN. Homemade formulas containing vinegar, baking soda and borax (sodium borate) will clean most of the house. To make laundry and dish soaps, add washing soda and soap flakes to the list.

BRING YOUR OWN BAGS TO THE GROCERY STORE. Canvas bags or the paper bags from your last trip to the market are a great reusable answer to the question of "Paper or plastic?" Many grocery stores offer customers a nickel discount for bringing and reusing bags.

READ LABELS ON HOUSEHOLD PAPER PRODUCTS. Purchase items such as paper towels and toilet paper that contain post-consumer content. This means recycled paper— not trees—was used to make the item. Its post-consumer content is the best measure of a product's impact on the environment.

COURTESY OF WHOLE FOODS MARKET WHOLEFOODS.COM

All About Organic...

WHAT IS ORGANIC?
Organic refers to the way agricultural products—food and fiber—are grown and processed. Organic food production is based on a system of farming that maintains and replenishes soil fertility without the use of toxic and persistent pesticides and fertilizers. Organic foods are minimally processed without artificial ingredients, preservatives, or irradiation to maintain the integrity of the food.

IS THERE AN OFFICIAL DEFINITION OF "ORGANIC"?
The following excerpt is from the definition of "organic" that the National Organic Standards Board adopted in April 1995: "Organic agriculture is an ecological production management system that promotes and enhances biodiversity, biological cycles and soil biological activity. It is based on minimal use of off-farm inputs and on management practices that restore, maintain and enhance ecological harmony."

WHAT DOES "CERTIFIED ORGANIC" MEAN?
"Certified Organic" means the item has been grown according to strict uniform standards that are verified by independent state or private organizations. Certification includes inspections of farm fields and processing facilities, detailed record keeping, and periodic testing of soil and water to ensure that growers and handlers are meeting the standards which have been set.

ARE ORGANICALLY GROWN FOODS BETTER FOR YOU? Organically grown foods are certainly better for our environment, and what's good for the environment is good for us. However, nutritionally speaking, you may not find a measurable difference between eating a conventionally grown carrot versus an organically grown carrot.

HOW IS ORGANIC PROCESSING BETTER FOR THE ENVIRONMENT? Organic farming, by definition, does not use environmentally harmful chemicals that may contaminate rain and groundwater. It also replenishes and maintains healthy, fertile topsoil with rich biological matter, which does not erode into waterways.

IS "NATURAL" THE SAME AS "ORGANIC"? The term "natural" often is misrepresented in product labeling to imply "healthful," but it only means the product has undergone minimal processing. Unlike certified organic products, natural products have no certification or inspection requirements. Also, "natural" does not necessarily relate to growing methods or use of preservatives.

SUPPORTING SUSTAINABILITY

Produce Selection & Storage Tips ...

APPLES
Any variety of apple should have a firm skin with no bruises. Store in the refrigerator to maximize freshness and flavor.

AVOCADOS
Look for dark even-colored avocadoes. Instead of squeezing to check for ripeness, pull the bud – if it comes off easily, it is ripe. Avocadoes ripen best when stored at 70 degrees but should be stored on a plate in the refrigerator to avoid bumps and bruises.

BANANAS
Look for the brightest colored yellow bananas you can find. Store at room temperature.

BELL PEPPERS
Peppers should be firm and even-colored and can be stored in the refrigerator or on the countertop.

BLUEBERRIES
Open up the container and look for even-colored berries, and insist on sampling before you leave the supermarket. Fresh blueberries will have a little fine white wax "bloom" on them with crowns that are fresh and standing up. Store in the coldest, driest part of your refrigerator.

CARROTS
Look for fresh, firm carrots with no black pockets. Carrots should last three weeks in the refrigerator.

GRAPES
Like berries, taste a grape before buying. Store at room temperature and wash just prior to eating.

LEMONS
Seek deep, rich yellow color and store on the counter for juicier lemons. Storing in the refrigerator will extend freshness, but let it sit out a day before using.

LETTUCE
Check for crispness. If lettuce is too crisp, it can easily bruise and be more difficult to work with. Always store in the refrigerator in the crisper.

LIMES
More perishable than lemons, smaller limes are juicier and should be stored at room temperature.

PEARS
Bartletts are the only variety that will turn mushy. Store all pears in the refrigerator. Place in a brown paper bag to ripen.

RASPBERRIES
The sweetest raspberries are soft – but not mushy. Enjoy soon after bringing home.

SCALLIONS
Scallions should be free of dirt and will last longer when stored in the refrigerator.

STRAWBERRIES
Inhale and enjoy the aroma of fresh strawberries, which should have a nice fresh, firm cap! Store in the berries' original packaging and only cut off the caps if brown spots appear. Use within a day or two of purchasing.

TOMATOES
Tomatoes should be firm, ripe and a deep red color. A fresh aroma is a plus! Avoid green tomatoes if possible. Store on the countertop but not in the refrigerator, and avoid direct sunlight. A fresh, ripe tomato should stay fresh for up to 5 days.

COURTESY OF WHOLE FOODS MARKET   WHOLEFOODS.COM

Clean & Green ...

Back in our great-grandparents' day, deciding what to use to clean up around the house was easy: soap, water and a little elbow grease. Today we're bombarded with an overwhelming array of products to scrub and polish our way to a sparkling clean home. Unfortunately, household cleaning products can contain many chemicals and toxins. Anyone looking for an alternative to national brands can easily make their own cleaning concoctions at home with these simple recipes with ingredients you already have in your cabinets.

OVEN CLEANER: Make a paste of equal parts salt, baking soda and water. First, wipe away any grease and scratch off burnt spots with a scouring brush or steel wool. Finally, apply the paste, let stand five minutes and wipe clean with a damp rag. Scrub if necessary. Do not allow baking soda to touch heating elements or wiring.

WOOD FLOOR POLISH: Mix 1/2 cup vinegar and 1/2 cup vegetable oil. Rub on floor and buff with a clean, dry cloth.

MOLD REMOVER: Saturate a sponge with vinegar and scrub the moldy area. Rinse well.

GLASS CLEANER: Combine 1/4 cup vinegar and one quart of water. Plain club soda also works!

MULTIPURPOSE CLEANER: Combine 1 teaspoon borax, 1 teaspoon baking soda, 2 teaspoons vinegar, 1/4 teaspoon dishwashing liquid, 1 teaspoon lemon juice and 2 cups hot water.

HEAVY-DUTY DISINFECTANT: Combine 1/4 cup powdered laundry detergent, 1-tablespoon borax, 3/4 cup hot water and 1/4 cup pine oil. Slowly stir the detergent and borax into the water to dissolve. Add the pine oil (available at hardware stores and supermarkets) and mix well.

CARPET FRESHENER: In a container with a tight-fitting lid, combine 1 cup crushed dried herbs (such as lavender or rosemary) with 1 teaspoon ground cloves, 1 teaspoon ground cinnamon and 2 teaspoons baking soda. Shake well to blend. Sprinkle the mixture on carpet and let sit for one hour. Vacuum.

TOILET BOWL CLEANER: Combine 1-cup borax with 1/4 cup vinegar or lemon juice to make a paste. Apply it to the inside of the toilet bowl and let it sit for 1 to 2 hours before scrubbing.

RUST REMOVER: Sprinkle salt on the rust and then squeeze a lime over the salt until it is soaked in juice. Let the mixture sit for up to three hours. The leftover lime rind can be used as a handy scrubber to remove the rust. Another option is to rub the rust with balled-up aluminum foil after wetting it with water. Use caution as aluminum foil will scratch chrome.

DRAIN CLEARING AGENT: Sprinkle a generous amount of baking soda in and around the drain opening. Follow with 1 cup of white vinegar. Repeat if necessary and flush with hot water.

TILE FLOOR CLEANERS: Mop floor with solution of 1 to 2 teaspoons of liquid dish soap dissolved in 3 gallons of warm water. Rinse with 1 cup of white vinegar in 3 gallons of cool water.

GREASE STAIN REMOVER: Cover stain with a mixture of borax and water. Rub in and wipe off. Rinse well after applying stain remover.

NATURAL LAUNDRY BLEACH: The only ingredients are 1/4 cup of lemon juice and some sunshine! Use the lemon juice in the washing machine's rinse cycle. After clothes have spun, hang in the sun to dry.

WALL AND WALLPAPER CLEANER: Dissolve 1/4 cup borax in 1 gallon hot water. Stir to blend. Use a sponge or rag.

SILVER CLEANER: Rub the silver with toothpaste; wipe off tarnish and then rinse. Dry with a soft cloth.

KITCHEN DISPOSAL FRESHENER: Just drop in a few lemon wedges and flip the switch.

COURTESY OF WHOLE FOODS MARKET   WHOLEFOODS.COM

Supporting Sustainability

Sustainable Seafood ...

The simple fact is our oceans are in trouble. Our world's fish stocks are disappearing from our seas because they have been over fished or harvested using damaging fishing practices. To keep our favorite seafood plentiful for us to enjoy and to keep it around for future generations, we must act now.

As a shopper, you have the power to turn the tide. When you purchase seafood from fisheries using ocean-friendly methods, you reward their actions and encourage other fisheries to operate responsibly.

HERE IS AN EASY TO FOLLOW GUIDE TO HELP YOU MAKE SUSTAINABLE SEAFOOD CHOICES:

BEST CHOICES: HEALTHY FISH STOCKS

FARMED CLAMS, MUSSELS, OYSTERS, AND BAY SCALLOPS FROM NORTH AMERICA
Shellfish filter feed and don't require fishmeal and fish oil for food. When farmed using suspended bags, nets, or cages—as opposed to being dredged—mollusks top our list of acceptable seafood.

ALASKA SALMON
With good management and fairly healthy habitat, Alaska salmon remain abundant. There are concerns that hatchery programs adversely affect wild salmon populations.

STRIPED BASS, WILD AND FARMED
Striped Bass are wild-caught and also farmed. Effective fisheries management helped wild Striped Bass recover from severe depletion in the 1980s to high abundance today. Farming hybrid Striped Bass results in few escapes and minimal pollution. However, their feed contains high amounts of fishmeal and fish oil.

MAHIMAHI, POLE- AND TROLL-CAUGHT
Mahimahi grow fast, live short lives and withstand high fishing pressure. Pole and troll fisheries catch Mahimahi with little bycatch compared to longline fisheries.

ALBACORE, BIGEYE, YELLOWFIN, AND SKIPJACK TUNA, POLE- AND TROLL-CAUGHT
Tunas are fast-growing, prolific breeders, and wide-ranging, but many populations are experiencing depletion. The low bycatch associated with pole- and troll-caught tuna makes them better alternatives to longline- or purse-seine-caught tuna.

AMERICAN LOBSTER, MAINE AND CANADA
Maine and Canadian lobster populations today thrive at record-high abundance. However, North Atlantic Right Whales, an endangered species, still become entangled in lobster fishing gear, a problem that raises significant concerns.

SQUID
Squid often reproduce before turning one year old and live short lives, characteristics that help them withstand high fishing pressure. The difficulty of managing squid fisheries lies in their sensitivity to changes in environmental conditions.

PACIFIC SOLES
Well-managed, these flatfish are currently abundant. However, bycatch and habitat damage from bottom trawling cause concern. Fishery managers try to minimize these impacts, especially where soles share habitat with depleted Pacific coast rockfish.

DUNGENESS*, KING, AND STONE CRABS
These crab species are fairly abundant thanks to wise management. High fertility helps Dungeness and Stone Crabs withstand fishing pressure. King Crabs brood their eggs for a year, making them vulnerable to fishing pressure. Crab fishers use relatively low-bycatch traps (or pots).

CATFISH, U.S.-FARMED
Fish farmers raise catfish in the southern U.S. in large earthen ponds, resulting in some water pollution. But escapes are rare, and catfish require much less fishmeal and fish oil in their feed than other farmed fish.

TILAPIA, U.S.-FARMED
Tilapia require little fishmeal and fish oil in their feed. U.S. tilapia farms produce less pollution than foreign farms. However, because tilapia are not native to the U.S., escapes that do occur
jeopardize native fish populations.

PACIFIC COD
While faring better than their Atlantic counterparts, Pacific Cod persist at only a moderate level of abundance. Managers limit catches and account for bycatch. Declines of marine mammals and bycatch of North Pacific albatrosses raise concerns about this fishery's ecosystem impacts.

PACIFIC HALIBUT
Although they grow slowly and can live over 50 years, Pacific Halibut remain abundant due to responsible management. Fishers own shares of the total annual catch, eliminating the dangerous incentive to fish competitively. Accidental deaths of seabirds, especially North Pacific albatrosses, concern the international commission that oversees this fishery.

SPECIES TO AVOID:

ATLANTIC COD
Decades of overfishing have driven Atlantic Cod populations to historic low levels. Even with heavy management, populations show no sign of rebuilding. Catch methods for Atlantic Cod—primarily bottom trawling—destroy habitat.

SHARKS
Many shark species are depleted worldwide. Sharks grow slowly and have few young. Poor management has made shark populations victims of widespread overfishing and bycatch. Sharks swim past national boundaries, yet no international management exists.

SHRIMP, IMPORTED
Bottom trawls used to catch most wild shrimp damage habitat and unintentionally kill many unwanted invertebrates, fish, and sea turtles. Coastal shrimp farming ruins life-supporting ecosystems such as mangroves and causes water pollution. Shrimp from the U.S. are generally better monitored and regulated. For more information on shrimp.

FARMED (ATLANTIC) SALMON
High environmental costs of farming salmon include water pollution, spread of diseases to wild populations, high content of wild fish in feed, and overuse of antibiotics. Wild Atlantic Salmon in the U.S. are endangered. Farms supply all Atlantic Salmon sold in the U.S.

GROUPERS
Generally long-lived, many groupers change sex with age and groupspawn in the same places every year, making them vulnerable to overfishing. Most groupers sold in the U.S. are imported, generally from countries with little management.

ORANGE ROUGHY
Orange Roughy don't mature until they're at least 20 years old, can live over 100 years, and are severely depleted. They live in deep waters where habitat-damaging trawls catch them when they gather in groups to feed or spawn. A number of deep-sea shark species caught as bycatch in Orange Roughy fisheries are threatened.

CHILEAN SEABASS
Really named Patagonian Toothfish, high demand for this naturally longlived fish drives depletion and creates an incentive for continued illegal fishing. Incidental catch of albatrosses and petrels.

ACCEPTABLE CHOICES, BUT KNOW WHERE IT COMES FROM—SOME STOCKS ARE OVERFISHED OR THREATENED

ALBACORE, BIGEYE, YELLOWFIN, AND SKIPJACK TUNA, CANNED OR LONGLINE-CAUGHT
Despite having naturally high fertility and wide ranges, many Albacore Tuna ("chunk white") and Bigeye, Yellowfin, and Skipjack Tuna ("chunk light") populations are declining from heavy fishing pressure. Globally, few regulations exist for tuna fisheries. Longline and purse-seine fishers catch large numbers of marine mammals, sea turtles, sharks, and young tunas. Despite U.S. "Dolphin Safe" standards for the canned tuna market, affected dolphins are not recovering.

MONKFISH
Monkfish are typically caught along with other groundfish such as Atlantic Cod and Haddock in the Northeast U.S. This fishery suffers from historically poor management, resulting in overfishing, depletion, and job losses. Gillnets and trawls, which cause high bycatch, catch the majority of Monkfish in the U.S. market.

SEA SCALLOPS
Wild Sea Scallops have recovered from being overfished, but current management measures allow too high fishing pressure and are controversial. Bottom dredges and trawls used to catch Sea Scallops damage habitat, and there is unintended catch of endangered sea turtles and depleted Atlantic Cod and other groundfish.

RAINBOW TROUT
Some problems with farming this species exist. Rainbow Trout feed contains large amounts of fishmeal and fish oil. However water pollution and other ecological risks of farming Rainbow Trout are low.

SWORDFISH
Swordfish remain overfished in the North Atlantic but show signs of recovery with stronger catch regulations. Their abundance appears high in the North Pacific, but their status is unclear in other parts of the Pacific. Most Swordfish are longline-caught, with high bycatch of albatrosses, sea turtles, and sharks.

SUPPORTING SUSTAINABILITY

FISH KEY
- Species is relatively abundant, and fishing/farming methods cause little damage to habitat and other wildlife.
- Some problems exist with this species' status or catch/farming methods, or information is insufficient for evaluating.
- Species has a combination of problems such as overfishing, high bycatch, and poor management, or farming methods have serious environmental impacts.

Information Courtesy of BLUE OCEAN.

FOR MORE INFORMATION, SEE BLUEOCEAN.ORG/SEAFOOD

TO LEARN MORE ABOUT SAFE SEAFOOD CHOICES FOR YOUR KIDS, VISIT KIDSAFESEAFOOD.ORG

Resources...

RESTAURANTS

MODERN MEXICAN RESTAURANTS
MODERNMEXICAN.COM — ACROSS THE GLOBE

MICHAEL MINA RESTAURANTS
MICHAELMINA.NET — ACROSS THE COUNTRY

MARCEL'S RESTAURANT
MARCELSDC.COM — WASHINGTON, D.C.

BRASSERIE BECK
BECKDC.COM — WASHINGTON, D.C.

TOWN HALL RESTAURANT
TOWNHALLSF.COM — SAN FRANCISCO, CA

NORTH POND RESTAURANT
NORTHPONDRESTAURANT.COM — CHICAGO, ILLINOIS

JOSEPH'S TABLE
JOSEPHSTABLE.COM — TAOS, NEW MEXICO

RESTAURANT EVE
RESTAURANTEVE.COM — ALEXANDRIA, VIRGINIA

EAMONNS DUBLIN CHIPPER
EAMONNSDUBLINCHIPPER.COM — ALEXANDRIA, VIRGINIA

DRISKILL GRILL
DRISKILLGRILL.COM — AUSTIN, TEXAS

RESTAURANT AUGUST
RESTAURANTAUGUST.COM — NEW ORLEANS, LOUISIANA

LUKE
LUKENEWORLEANS.COM — NEW ORLEANS, LOUISIANA

CHEF MICHEL NISCHAN
MICHELNISCHAN.COM — LEARN MORE FROM THE CHEF

DRESSING ROOM RESTAURANT
DRESSINGROOMHOMEGROWN.COM — WESTPORT, CONNECTICUT

TELEPAN RESTAURANT
TELEPAN-NY.COM — NEW YORK, NEW YORK

CRUSH RESTAURANT
CHEFJASONWILSON.COM — SEATTLE, WASHINGTON

FOR MORE INFORMATION AND RESOURCES, VISIT CHEFSAFIELD.COM

FARMERS, FISHERMEN, RANCHERS, GROWERS & RESOURCES

AVOCADOS FROM MEXICO
  AVOCADOSFROMMEXICO.COM   ALL ABOUT AVOCADOS

CALIFORNIA WALNUTS
  WALNUTS.ORG   ALL ABOUT WALNUTS

CALIFORNIA STRAWBERRIES
  CALSTRAWBERRY.COM   ALL ABOUT

PRIME SEAFOOD
  PRIMESEAFOOD.COM   KENSINGTON, MARYLAND

FANTOME FARM
  FANTOMEFARM.COM   RIDGEWAY, WISCONSIN

SEEDS OF CHANGE
  SEEDSOFCHANGE.COM   AVAILABLE NATION-WIDE

POLYFACE FARMS
  POLYFACEFARMS.COM   SWOOPE, VIRGINIA

BROKEN ARROW RANCH
  BROKENARROWRANCH.COM   INGRAM, TEXAS

LOUISIANA SHRIMPERS
  WHITEBOOTBRIGADE.ORG   THROUGHOUT LOUISIANA

TAYLOR CULTURED SHELLFISH
  RODMANTAYLOR@AOL.COM   FAIRHAVEN, MASSACHUSETTES

RONNYBROOK FARM
  RONNYBROOK.COM   ANCRAMDALE, NEW YORK

SEAFOOOD CHOICES ALLIANCE
  SEAFOODCHOICES.ORG   SEAFOOD CHOICES MADE EASY

KID SAFE SEAFOOD
  KIDSAFESEAFOOD.ORG   WHAT SEAFOOD IS SAFE FOR KIDS

SEAWEB
  SEAWEB.ORG   SUSTAINABLE SEAFOOD RESOURCE

BLUE OCEAN INSTITUTE
  BLUEOCEAN.ORG   ALL ABOUT OUR OCEANS

LOUISIANA SEAFOOD
  LOUISIANASEAFOOD.COM   LEARN ABOUT SHRIMP

EAT WILD
  EATWILD.COM   LEARN MORE

LOCAL HARVEST
  LOCALHARVEST.ORG   FIND A FARMER

KIMPTON HOTEL GROUP
  KIMPTON.COM   ECO-FRIENDLY ACCOMMODATIONS

WHOLE FOODS MARKET
  WHOLEFOODS.COM   LOCATIONS NATION-WIDE

People & Places

The Sponsors ...

CHEFS A' FIELD: KIDS ON THE FARM IS MADE POSSIBLE BY THE GENEROUS SUPPORT OF OUR SPONSORS.

MAJOR CORPORATE SPONSOR:

WHOLE FOODS MARKET. WHOLE PEOPLE. WHOLE PLANET. WHOLE FOODS.

WHOLE FOODS MARKET

Founded in 1980 in Austin, Texas, WHOLE FOODS MARKET is the world's leading natural and organic foods supermarket and America's first national certified organic grocer. In fiscal year 2006, the company had sales of $5.6 billion and currently has more than 190 stores in the United States, Canada, and the United Kingdom. The Whole Foods Market motto, "Whole Foods, Whole People, Whole Planet"™ captures the company's mission to find success in customer satisfaction and wellness, employee excellence and happiness, enhanced shareholder value, community support and environmental improvement. Whole Foods Market, Harry's Farmers Market®, and Fresh & Wild® are trademarks owned by Whole Foods Market IP, LP. Whole Foods Market employs more than 41,500 team members and has been ranked for ten consecutive years as one of the "100 Best Companies to Work For" in America by FORTUNE magazine.

FOR MORE INFORMATION ABOUT WHOLE FOODS MARKET, VISIT WHOLEFOODS.COM

ADDITIONAL SUPPORT FOR THE SERIES AND ITS EDUCATIONAL OUTREACH ARE PROVIDED BY:

FULL CIRCLE FOOD
Discover! the goodness of Full Circle, an abundance of opportunities for you and your family to eat well & live well...Enjoy! great taste, naturally, that allows you and your family to eat well ... and live well. Celebrate! freedom from preservatives, artificial ingredients and other additives that mask natural goodness ... Full Circle Food is a a division of premium organic foods from Topco Associates. Available at your local grocer.
FOR MORE INFORMATION, VISIT FULLCIRCLEFOODS.COM

SEEDS OF CHANGE
In 1989, we at Seeds of Change started with a simple mission: to help preserve biodiversity and promote sustainable, organic agriculture. We sought to do this by cultivating and disseminating an extensive range of open-pollinated, organically grown, heirloom and traditional vegetable, flower and herb seeds. This is still our mission.
FOR MORE INFORMATION, VISIT SEEDSOFCHANGE.COM

THE PARK FOUNDATION
The Park Foundation was established by the late Roy Hampton Park, Sr. — founder, chairman, and chief executive officer of Park Communications, Inc. Roy Park led his life by a simple tenet: "Look for opportunity more than security and stability. Consider the breadth of an opportunity and do your best." The Foundation is dedicated to the aid and support of education, public broadcasting, environment, and other selected areas of interest to the Park family.
FOR MORE INFORMATION, VISIT PARKFOUNDATION.ORG

WALLACE GENETIC FOUNDATION
"The greatest private pleasure comes from serving the general welfare of all ..." --Henry A. Wallace. The Wallace Genetic Foundation is committed to funding a variety of interests including agricultural research, preservation of farmland, ecology, conservation and sustainable development
FOR MORE INFORMATION, VISIT WALLACEGENETIC.ORG

CALIFORNIA STRAWBERRY COMMISSION
The California Strawberry Commission is a state government agency that represents an industry of approximately 510 California strawberry growers and 75 shippers and processors. The Commission was enacted by enabling legislation and a referendum of farmers and handlers in 1993, succeeding the California Strawberry Advisory Board, which was established in 1955. California Strawberry Commission is an educational and outreach partner to *Chefs A' Field*.
FOR MORE INFORMATION, VISIT CALSTRAWBERRY.COM

WALNUT MARKETING BOARD
The Walnut Marketing Board was established in 1933 to represent the walnut growers and handlers of California. The Board is funded by mandatory assessments of the handlers. The WMB is governed by a Federal Walnut Marketing Order. The Board promotes usage of walnuts in the United States through publicity and educational programs. The Board also provides funding for walnut production and post-harvest research. Walnut Marketing Board is an educational and outreach partner to *Chefs A' Field*.
FOR MORE INFORMATION, VISIT WALNUTS.ORG

SPOONS ACROSS AMERICA
Spoons Across America,® the source for children's culinary education is a not-for-profit organization dedicated to educating children, teachers, and families about the benefits of healthy eating. We work to influence the eating habits of children through hands-on education that celebrates the connection to local farmers and the important tradition of sharing meals around the family table.
FOR MORE INFORMATION, VISIT SPOONSACROSSAMERICA.ORG

P E O P L E & P L A C E S

People & Places 155

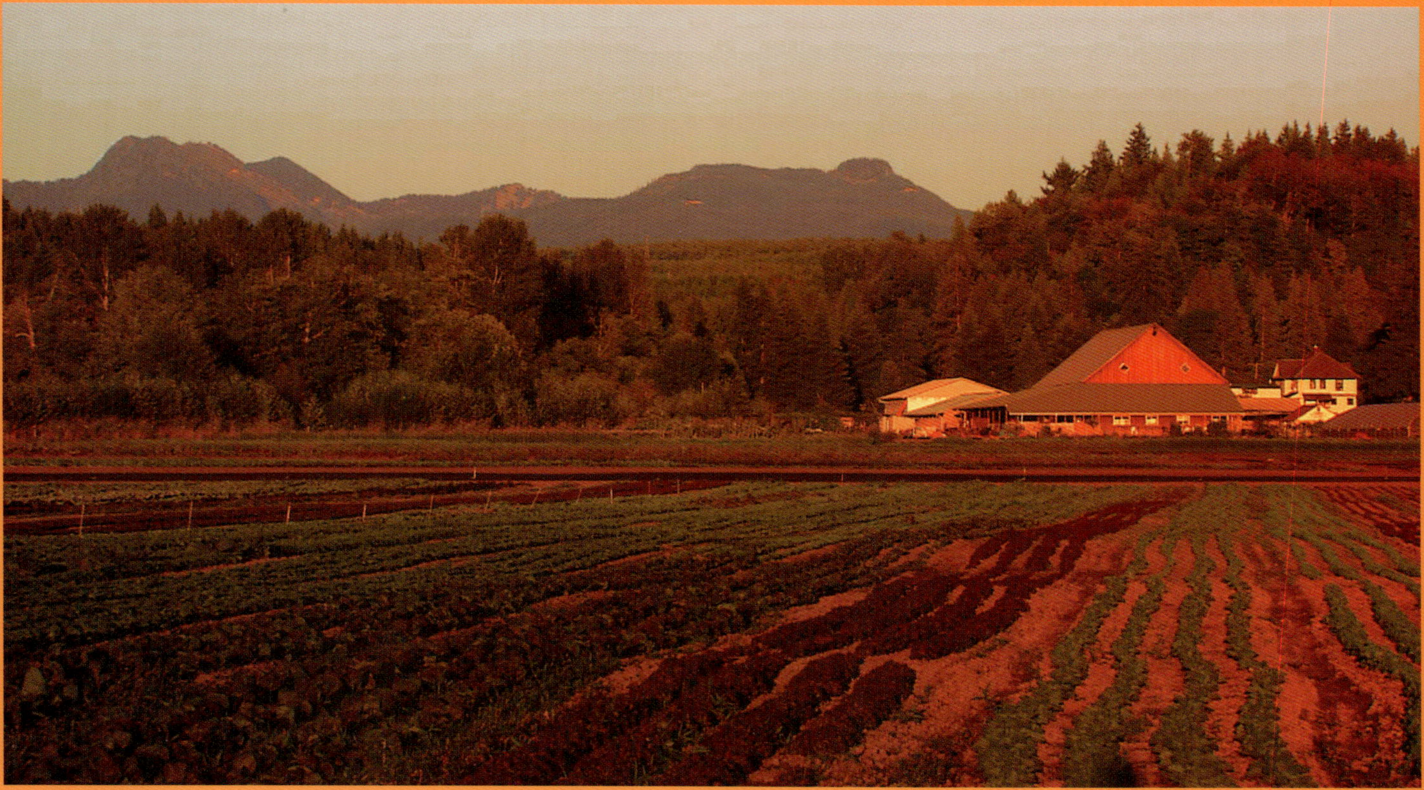

Producers...

CHEFS A' FIELD IS A CO-PRODUCTION OF WARNER HANSON TELEVISION & KCTS TELEVISION.

WARNER HANSON TELEVISION

WARNER HANSON TELEVISION (WHTV) produces film and television programs on subjects such as wildlife, natural history, and the environment for major television networks nationally and abroad. Respected producers of quality documentary programs and specialists in High Definition Television (HDTV), WHTV has filmed in some of world's most remote areas of North and South America, Africa, Asia, and Iceland.

WHTV's latest effort, the critically acclaimed 39-part series *Chefs A' Field*, is seen nationally on Public Television. The series was the nation's first cooking series to be produced in HDTV (1080i).

WHTV is also in production on several national series focusing on wildlife, sustainability, and natural history. Their work also includes current news magazine and news coverage that airs on ABC, PBS, BBC, ABC, Discovery, OLN, and other channels. Film footage from the WHTV library has appeared on CSI, The West Wing, Commander In Chief, and other theatrical releases.

WHTV produces television programs, exhibits, and films for non-broadcast clients that include: Smithsonian Institution, The Nature Conservancy, US Dept. of Education, US Dept. of Agriculture, National Cancer Institute, US Holocaust Memorial Museum, and others. WHTV has received numerous awards, including multiple CINE Golden Eagle Awards, James Beard Foundation Awards, White House News Photographers Awards, the Dei Popoli Jury Award, and Telly Awards.

Chefs A' Field Credits:
   Writer / Narrator: Jed Duvall
   Directors of Photography: Tim Murray, Mark Thalman, Rich Joy, Chris Warner
   Field Audio: Juan Rocha
   Post-Production: Ventana Productions
   Producer: Heidi Hanson
   Executive Producer: Chris Warner
   Chefs A' Field was created by Warner Hanson Television.

FOR MORE INFORMATION ABOUT WARNER HANSON TELEVISION, VISIT WARNERHANSON.COM.

KCTS/SEATTLE PUBLIC TELEVISION

KCTS/SEATTLE PUBLIC TELEVISION serves viewers by producing and presenting quality information and entertainment programs that reflect its mission to "*inform, involve and inspire.*"

KCTS has created numerous award-winning programs, series and prime-time specials that have aired on public television, cable and commercial networks. In the last decade alone, the station has received nearly 200 awards in recognition of a wide range of production activities serving the needs of local, national and international audiences.

KCTS' production credits include such popular how-to series as *Chefs A' Field, Nick Stellino's Family Kitchen's Family Kitchen* and *Graham Kerr's Gathering Place*; six seasons of the award-winning series *Bill Nye the Science Guy®*; the Emmy-nominated series *The Perilous Fight: America's World War II in Color*; the PBS specials *The Video Game Revolution, Inside Passage and Exploring Space*; and the series *The Eyes of Nye*.

FOR MORE INFORMATION ABOUT KCTS, VISIT KCTS.ORG

CHEFS A' FIELD IS DISTRIBUTED BY AMERICAN PUBLIC TELEVISION

FOR MORE INFORMATION ABOUT APT, VISIT APTONLINE.ORG

CHEFSAFIELD.COM

WARNER
HANSON
TELEVISION

WASHINGTON DC

WARNERHANSON.COM

KCTS
SEATTLE

KCTS.ORG